Theology, Liberatio [illegible] nocide

RECLAIMING LIBERATION THEOLOGY

Theology, Liberation and Genocide

Mario I. Aguilar

scm press

Published in 2009 by SCM Press
Editorial office
13–17 Long Lane,
London, EC1A 9PN, UK

SCM Press is an imprint of Hymns Ancient and Modern Ltd
(a registered charity)
St Mary's Works, St Mary's Plain,
Norwich, NR3 3BH, UK
www.scm-canterburypress.co.uk

British Library Cataloguing in Publication data

A catalogue record for this book is available from the British Library

978 0 334 04190 0

Typeset by Regent Typesetting, London
Printed and bound by
CPI Antony Rowe, Chippenham SN14 6LH

Contents

To the memory of Marcella Althaus-Reid

(+2009)

An outstanding theologian, a committed activist and a friend
who inspired and encouraged this work

Y se abrirán las grandes alamedas donde caminen el hombre y la mujer libres . . .

To the memory of my father Mario Aguilar Letelier

(+1996)

¡Te eché de menos toda la vida y ya te fuiste!

Acknowledgements

Every book is like an empty canvas, a tapestry on which choices of subject, colour, style and aesthetic narrative are the choice of the artist. However, during the time in which the artist works and recreates the canvas or the page he is influenced by people, beauty, suffering and life that surround him. Thus, my acknowledgements are to those who have made this process of filling this particular canvas fruitful, painful, controversial and even personal.

A small part of this theological canvas is an expansion and reinterpretation of arguments previously rehearsed. Thus, Chapter 3 is an extended revised version of 'Public Theology from the Periphery: Victims and Theologians', *International Journal of Public Theology* 1, 2007, pp. 321–37, and Chapter 4 is a revised version of arguments previously outlined in 'Postcolonial African Theology in Kabasele Lumbala', *Theological Studies* 63, 2002, pp. 302–23.

This book is dedicated to the late Argentinean theologian Marcella Althaus-Reid who died in her intellectual prime in 2009. Marcella was a wonderfully creative, beautiful and warm person who encouraged my writings on Latin American theology after she invited me to give a public lecture on the subject at the University of Edinburgh in 2005. Marcella, rest in peace but continue the *caminata* with us.

This book is also dedicated to my late father, Mario Aguilar Letelier (+1996). I met him only once after I was a child and I longed for years to know where he was, what he was like, what we could talk about etc. As I was completing this book, I learned from my sister Loreto that he died in 1996 and is buried at his home town of Constitución, Chile. I dedicate this book to his memory as I have learned over the past weeks how much he remembered me throughout his life as well. Several people I knew have died during the past few months, but the news that I would never have the chance to talk to my father gave me a heavy heart. May he rest in peace as well!

My thanks go to Natalie Watson, Senior Commissioning Editor at SCM Press, who entertained the idea of this book and had to wait for the manuscript a bit longer than anticipated. The completion of the manuscript was greatly helped by friends in Chile and I thank Glenda Tello, Santiago Hunfán, René Acevedo, Máximo G. Sáez, Elías Padilla, Verónica Ibáñez and Fesal Chain for their ongoing support and friendship.

As usual I thank colleagues at St Mary's College of the University of St Andrews for creating a convivial and intellectually stimulating atmosphere in which to discuss ideas and developments in theology. I thank particularly Dr Eric Stoddart and my current doctoral students Alissa Jones Nelson, Yumi Murayama, Rob Whiteman, Casey Nicholson, Gordon Barclay and Mary Stevens.

Santiago, Chile
March 2009

Introduction

Theologizing at the Periphery

Theology, liberation and genocide: what is the connection between these three concepts? I follow here Jung Mo Sung, who in his latest work translated into English, argues 'it is precisely for that not being very common that this book explicitly attempts to approach the logic that interlinks the three words', referring in his case to desire, market and religion.[1] In liberation theology, it has been unusual to theologize about an absent God or about the silence of God. Therefore, in this work, I want to explore what liberation theologians in Latin America, Africa or Asia have not done. For, despite the fact that poverty, suffering and violence were the central social realities and social themes of engagement by liberation theologians of the first generation, the only engagement with the 'negation' or absence of God came through the dialogue between José Míguez Bonino, Christians and Marxists in the Argentinean context of the 1970s and 1980s.[2] After all, theologies of liberation arose out of the overwhelming response to suffering, poverty and oppression by Christian communities, filled with God, and triggered by the theological reflections of educated theologians that provided a 'second step' to praxis as 'the first step'.[3] I myself have to recognize that my theological presupposition of 'faith seeking understanding' has also prevented me from dealing with 'the absence of God' or 'the death of God' as markers of hermeneutical significance in my work so far.[4]

I maintain in this work that following the encouragement of Iván Petrella and his proposed engagement with all disciplines, all subjects and all contexts, liberating theology as a theologizing from the side of the poor must engage with a phenomenon previously considered European: the absence or silence of God in times of war, ethnic cleansing or genocide.[5] If, after World War Two, European theologians had to engage with the possibility of 'the absence of God' in Auschwitz and other Nazi extermination camps, I propose that it is impossible to continue theologizing about poverty and suffering in the Third and Fourth Worlds without confronting the possible shift of God from the centre to the periphery during and after the 1994 Rwandan genocide. After

Rwanda, we cannot as liberation theologians blame solely the colonial powers or the Europeans for suffering and oppression, but must engage with the 'silence of God' in Rwanda as an antithesis of the hopeful realities of liberation, and we must revisit European discussions after the Holocaust in order to enjoy liberation from sin, both personal and social. Contemporary discussions and theological investigations require an ongoing common humanity in which the values of the kingdom of justice and peace, and above all equality, must be proclaimed through the service of the poor and the marginalized on the periphery of society in Latin America, Africa and Asia. It is very striking that at the end of her assessment of the Holocaust within twentieth-century theology, Rosemary Radford Ruether provided the same critical assessment stating that 'We must seek a theology and ethic of co-humanity that fosters a quest for mutual justice between neighbours who must learn to live together in one land and one earth'.[6]

In this book, I return to some of the themes I have developed previously in relation to Latin America in order to explore how to theologize with a liberationist streak within conditions of absolute despair, proposing that the past, present and future is related less to high theologies of reconciliation in Christ than to service, proclamation and solidarity with the poor and the marginalized, symbolized in the case of Rwanda by all, killers and victims, all members of the Body of Christ, who suffered not only the experience of a silent God but also the exodus of expatriate missionaries, desecration of churches and fragmentation of all that could be deemed holy, sacred and fully human. In my previous work on Rwanda, I tried to understand what happened and in my conclusion I expressed my failure to do so. In this work I affirm without apology the preferential option for the poor and the marginalized by a servant Church that follows God the Liberator. This takes second place to the God who was with the victims but with them remained silent and couldn't speak because church agents and those who were educated to defend life and to speak of God failed to do so. The triumphant Church fell silent and the church of the grassroots, of the courageous poor and marginalized managed to arise out of the cut limbs and heads of Christ in Rwanda. It is my thesis, once again, that as the first Christian communities arose out of an empty tomb and the blood of martyrs and those persecuted in the first three centuries of Christianity, the process of theologizing about Rwanda can become a marker of hope and solidarity for all communities and theologians working in the Third and the Fourth Worlds who face ongoing hardships, violence and discrimination together with the poor and the marginalized.

Rwandan Hopes and Aspirations

In November 2007, the Rwandan President Paul Kagame received an honorary doctorate from the University of Glasgow and on that festive occasion he delivered a public lecture on development in Rwanda. His material achievements cannot be doubted; Kagame managed to provide political leadership for a country devastated by the 1994 genocide, a period between April and July 1994 through which at least 1,117,000 people were killed at the hands of people they knew themselves.[7] The material and moral devastation of that event made any possibility of dreaming of a new Rwanda very difficult indeed. I am the first one to agree that Kagame implemented a very authoritarian regime and that the issue of human rights, punishment and reconciliation provided a challenge which will remain for more than a generation. However, despite those challenges there is a national project of nation-building, including education, health and international cooperation that has provided some utopian moments of liberation, hope and solidarity, previously unthinkable.

However, despite those positive signs of nation-building there is still a question mark regarding the actual events and communal actions that triggered the genocide as well as questions regarding the fact that most of those who killed were Christians but very few of them tried to impede the killings. Further, recent interviews with killers show that they took a break from God's orders in order to obey other leaders and that churches didn't function as places of shelter, worship or comfort.[8] As in the case of the Nazi concentration camps, it seemed that God had gone from the places of slaughter. In the words of a killer, 'They [the Tutsis] were abandoned by everything, even by God. They no longer spoke to Him at all.'[9] Further, another killer described the possibility and the actuality of their interruption of religious practices in the following words:

> The white priests took off at the first skirmishes. The black priests joined the killers or the killed. God kept silent, and the churches stank from abandoned bodies. Religion could not find its place in our activities. For a little while, we were no longer ordinary Christians, we had to forget our duties learned in catechism class. We had first of all to obey our leaders – and God only afterwards, very long afterwards, to make confession and penance. When the job was done.[10]

I shall return to Rwanda as a *locus theologicus* within the first part of this book. At this point, it is crucial to address the possibility that the experience of the genocide in Rwanda connects with theological reflection on the parameters and hermeneutics of liberation and liberation theology at a larger level. Within an emerging 'reclaiming of liberation theology' for the twenty-first century, the theological reflection from the point of view of 'the poor or the marginalized' of Rwanda becomes crucial for the theological reflection of liberation elsewhere and particularly throughout the Christian communities of Africa, Latin America, Asia, North America and Europe in a new theological dawn of God's liberation for his people. Throughout the colonial and post-colonial period, more Christians in Rwanda than in any other African country were born of the waters of baptism and the womb of the Catholic Church, yet Christians killed others on a massive scale, their hatred based on blood rather than the Trinitarian waters of the baptismal font.

Within that framework of ongoing development in a post-genocidal Rwanda two surprising phenomena replicate the experience of Christianity and liberation in other parts of the world: (1) the Rwandan administration under Kagame perceived 'religion' as the cause of the ethnic problem and not as the possible solution to the problem; and (2) ten years after the 1994 genocide the people of Rwanda continued filling the churches where victims had been killed in large numbers, and there were more baptisms and more vocations for the Catholic Church than before the genocide. If for the Rwandan government religion provided a problem for others, it is possible to argue that religion could provide a common sense of purpose, liberation and a solution to the ethnic problems. For, as Jung Mo Sung has written in his theology of the market, a desire for reconciliation, for Christian freedom and liberation for all seems to dominate the life of ordinary Rwandans who speak of 'the period of the troubles' as an example of past foolishness and social misunderstanding.

I am not concerned here with the means and ends of a just society, nor of a particular just Rwandan society, but with the possibility of utopian dreams and Christian utopias of liberation displacing consumerism. The market has been imposed by globalization with its fetishism of commodities conceived as extensions of the self. The Christian self, by contrast, is free within the context of a 'liberation Christianity'. So, in Sung's analysis,

> The suffering and death of the poor, to the extent that they are considered the other side of the coin of the 'redeeming progress', are interpreted as necessary sacrifices for this same progress. Misery and death are facts which, as is the case with all facts, are open to

diverse interpretations. Some interpret them as murder, and some as necessary sacrifices.[11]

This idea of 'necessary sacrifice' is applied by utopian African politicians in their dreams of the birth of a new nation or of social engineering that could avoid all problems of ethnic and linguistic diversity. It is my suggestion that after those challenging moments of hatred and killing, theologizing remains the liberating action that allows the poor and marginalized, particularly those who are members of Christian communities, to read history in terms of God's liberating actions, even at a time of annihilation and despair. God is a liberator not because of particular moments of liberation, for example the Exodus from Egypt, but because God desires liberation and freedom for all at all times even when he remains powerless and unable to stop the killing of a million baptized people in Rwanda. The process of theologizing becomes a human reflection by human agents providing a contrast to God's symphony of liberation.

Theological Shifts for the Twenty-First Century

Two of the greatest theological shifts over the past 40 years have been the displacement of Europe from the centre of world Christianity and the decline of metanarratives regarding the centrality of Christianity within European thought. Both shifts have been triggered by a process of secularization but have also featured theological questioning regarding suffering. For if the creation of wealth, consumerism and globalization have continued to regard pain and suffering as something to be controlled, the mere historical fact of the Shoah or the Holocaust or the mass gassing of Jews at Auschwitz has made theological reflection more tentative and has divided theologians, particularly Jewish theologians, into those who could not believe in a God after such atrocity and those who still maintained the existence of God after Auschwitz.

By the early 1990s, after the fall of the Berlin Wall, there was a new sense of optimism and indeed a revival of the possibility of a united and strong Europe that could have learned the lessons of World War Two as well as the lessons of the Cold War. And there came a new challenge to such romantic notion of postmodernist bliss: Rwanda. Between April and July 1994, an orchestrated genocidal machine killed almost one million Rwandans, labelled Tutsis by the Hutu, labelling that included those who were in mixed marriages and those who supported a system of politics without ethnic levelling who were later labelled as 'moderates'. The history of the Rwandan genocide seems to be an ongoing disaster in which the European colonial powers created a climate of ethnic division that led to bloodshed in Rwanda as soon as the oppressed majority had been given independence.

However, the tragedy and the challenge provided by the Rwandan genocide came from the fact that Rwanda had been one of the most successful grounds for missionary work and almost all the Rwandan population belonged to the same Christian tradition, the Catholic Church. They all spoke the same language and over the years intermarriage by significant numbers of the population had provided a kind of common life in a country that suffered from overpopulation and shortage of land and resources. As in the case of Auschwitz, questions can be asked about how so much suffering can be inflicted by human beings on other human beings. Further questions need to be asked about the fact that Catholics killed Catholics and that the Rwandan Church failed to protect those killed and to influence the international community as well as their own communities when organized gangs of politicians, soldiers and civilians gathered people in their thousands to slaughter them. Not only did relatives kill relatives but most of the victims were gathered and killed in churches, in schools and other places normally considered sacred. Finally, some priests and nuns facilitated the gathering of the faithful inside churches and some priests even took part in the killing, raping and torturing of the victims.

Most writings about the Rwandan genocide have condemned the silence of the international community at that moment; Christian theologians who have visited Rwanda have written about justice, reconciliation and the possibility of continuing being human in Rwanda. Thus, Mary Grey has insightfully explored issues of reconciliation and justice within Christianity and other religions that could provide understanding and further avenues for the Christian reflection in Rwanda and the assumption of guilt by a Church that failed completely.[12]

Indeed, issues of religion and its connections with governance and development remains a taboo subject due to the fact that for the Rwandan government of President Kagame the Catholic Church became too close to the colonial powers and as a result became part of the problem and not the solution. Nor does there seem to be an interest on the part of the Rwandan bishops in being directly involved with the government of the Rwanda Patriotic Front (RPF), the military group that in July 1994 marched into Rwanda from Uganda and managed to stop the genocide. The RPF has stabilized the country and introduced reforms that seem to be transforming Rwanda into a country with education and health facilities and that is wanted as economic partner by European donors and international organizations.

As a theologian who wrote an earlier work on Christianity in Rwanda, I cannot be satisfied with calls for reconciliation and for a common nationhood of all Rwandans without a call to strengthen a liberating Christianity of the grassroots. In my previous work, even when I failed to understand what happened to Catholics at the time of the genocide, I still maintained that 'Christian communities in Africa must keep their option for life, justice, peace, and unity against all odds'.[13] I also discovered cases of Catholic clergy and Catholic nuns who defended people and who in turn were killed for asserting the right to life of all human beings, in Rwanda and elsewhere. Ten years later, it is clear that the position of the Catholic Church has become peripheral to the nation state and that fresh theologizing is required now that 15 years have passed since the genocide. It is possible to start this process of theologizing by making a methodological statement and a sociological statement, both pertinent to my argument concerning the ongoing presence of God in Rwanda. There are signs of a development of kingdom-like attitudes in the post-genocidal period when a theology of the periphery and a hermeneutics of bones and skeletons is not only possible but central for theology.

A methodological consideration points to my previous work on a theology of the periphery: God moves to peripherical locations, sometimes outside any Christian community, in order to continue loving all human beings, Hutus and Tutsis, Rwandans and Europeans, victims and perpetrators of the genocide.[14] That theology of the periphery is a 'second act', thus requires the action of a community in the name of God first, a liberating praxis that loves first and reflects after. Within that process of Christian following and assertion of loving attitudes it is possible to argue that given the shocking atrocities that took place in Rwanda very few revenge killings or beatings have taken place and that Rwandans returned to their places of life and work with an enormous need to move on.

The sociological analysis of Rwanda today suggests that there are more vocations and baptisms in Rwanda than before the genocide and that the communities at grassroots level have been instrumental in bringing survivors and perpetrators together not only socially but in the church and in the villages of mostly rural Rwanda. If God wants to liberate, he will do so and his acts cannot be predicted on the basis of his association with a particular government. This can only be done through the questioning of any unjust social structures and any political mechanisms that could fuel ethnic and social divisions, social and economic inequality and the possibility of human development as the enrichment of a few within society to the detriment of others, and to the detriment of a majority that remains poor and marginalized. The possible strength of a reconciled Rwanda lies within the roots of a Christianity based on strong Christian communities, maybe not in numbers or social importance, but in commitment and solidarity with the poor and the marginalized, with the victims and the killer-victims of the genocide. The lessons of Rwanda are the lessons of a common humanity in which all of us can become killers and in which it is not possible to assure the international community that there will be no other genocides during the twenty-first century. Indeed, the transition from Kagame's government to other leadership could be difficult and traumatic for many Rwandans.

I would argue that the lessons of the Holocaust are quite similar to the lessons of Rwanda. The reconstruction of Germany created a very strong economic nation but at the same time a nation that tried to forget about the atrocities and crimes perpetrated by the Nazi regime. Those who lived through the Nazi period blamed the allies for the destruction of Germany and indeed the allied armies destroyed large cities in Germany in order to end Hitler's regime. Younger generations have examined the war and the Holocaust in a different light, blaming their own parents for not doing enough to prevent the rise of Nazism and the Holocaust. It is not my task to judge one or the other; however, I am very conscious that economic growth and development in Germany or in Rwanda requires the strong role of the Christian communities and indeed all of the faith communities if it is not going to be just a materialistic enterprise of nation-building.

It is here that the experience of the Rwandan people connects with that of other people throughout the world who have suffered. The strong solidarity with the poor and the marginalized represents a crucial movement towards preventing genocide, bringing liberation and living a life in community that follows the values of the Kingdom of God as proclaimed by Jesus of Nazareth, the Christ of faith within the Gospels. Mary Grey, in her book on Rwanda, provided a very thoughtful and warm response to her visit to a post-genocide Rwanda and searched theologically for the strength of the scriptures and the tradition in order to find tools for an ongoing reconciliation. I found her work very convincing, still very European-centred but helpful in connecting Third World theologies and the possibilities of central theological reflection. In a way that nobody else has attempted successfully, she argues for parameters of understanding of causation, a divine causation that sometimes cannot be understood. She writes, for example:

> the most profound reason for calling this path to reconciliation mystical lies in what has been revealed about the Trinitarian God. For Christians, God is hidden, *absconditus*, yet wonderfully revealed in the life and death of Christ, in the sacramental life of the Church that is not separated from Divine sacred presence in creation, but builds on this.[15]

However, in my own very, very tentative theological reading, reconciliation and the prevention of any ethnic cleansing of genocide only comes out of strong Christian communities within the context of a nation such as Rwanda where most citizens involved in the genocide were Christians. Thus, the failure of Rwanda was the failure to maintain local communities that could have prevented the genocide by speaking out in great numbers against the killings. It was the failure of most of the Rwandan bishops to exercise their power of alerting the international community and it was the failure of every Christian who killed others in contravention of the strongest commandment 'Thou shall not kill'.

Liberation Theology after Rwanda

However, this is not a book about theology in Rwanda because theology in Rwanda as a historical process ceases with the 1994 genocide. It freezes in time and space because God becomes frozen by the killings and by the thousands who routinely killed and returned to their homes after 'having done their job daily'. It is not a book about Rwanda because the experience of God in Rwanda is the experience of a failed understanding of what it is to be Christian, to be fully human and a child of God. That is a common factor in all the genocides, in all ethnic cleansings and killings that took place after the collapse of the Berlin Wall, a moment of utopian euphoria for a common humanity. That euphoria lasted for a very short time as the killings started in Bosnia, Rwanda, Somalia, the Democratic Republic of Congo and culminated with the age of 'terrorism' and 9/11 followed by extreme violence in Iraq and Afghanistan.

The theological questions about Rwanda become a heuristic methodology and a hermeneutical tool for all those involved in theologies of liberation after Rwanda. For the questions of Rwanda are not mainly about processes of possible reconciliation but about theological narratives that created the possibility of an ethnic discrimination during colonial times and the possibility that such discrimination in the name of a false conception of God could bring further killings, violence and unrest. The theological questions posed by Rwanda are the questions posed by any conflict within the excluded Third and Fourth Worlds where life is cheap and where a million killings attract no more attention than the killing of one single person or the kidnapping of another would create in any country of the rich and powerful G8.

This book is an attempt to widen theological participation within liberation narratives by widening the Latin American discussions of my previous work into two particular areas that remain unexplored within liberation theology. The first is the issue of the denial of God, deeply embedded in Marx and misunderstood in discussions of atheism; the second refers to hermeneutics and the centrality of the Christian hermeneutical project that precedes the discussions of postmodernity. If God seemed to be absent in Rwanda, that perceived absence had already been fuelled by Ludwig Feuerbach in the nineteenth century, creating a dynamics of creativity between theism and atheism, wrongly associated with Karl Marx.[16] And if Marx denied the possibility of God in human revolutionary changes, a point of encounter has been found with the mystical Christian traditions in which a dark journey of the soul takes place rather than an intellectual or emotional one.[17] If liberation theologians of the first and second generations did not pay attention to atheism or the absence of God because they thought that it was a northern preoccupation, this is the time to start asking theological questions about the denial of God in the southern hemisphere from the perspective of Rwanda. If existentialism and postmodernism seemed to be ignored by liberation theologians (because, again, they are phenomena associated with European individualism) this is the time to ask questions about the hermeneutics of bones after Rwanda because the European philosopher Gianni Vattimo has concluded the same that could be concluded for Rwanda: the essential trait of any theological journey and any hermeneutical journey is the possibility of differences between the theist and the atheist; however, in the end what makes both of them and each one of us human and Christian is the act of love and the common humanity, basic for Christian theological narratives of liberation theologians.

A Hermeneutics of Bones at the Periphery

Vattimo has argued for the primacy of love when after many years of philosophical investigations into belief, God, hermeneutics and postmodernism he paraphrases Benedetto Croce:

> We cannot call ourselves Christians because in a world where God is dead – where the metanarratives have been dissolved and all authority has fortunately been demythologized, including that of 'objective' knowledge – our only chance of human survival rests in the Christian commandment of charity.[18]

If a theological narrative of Rwanda becomes a common narrative of humanity's suffering and liberation, it will be because we recognize that social changes and processes of challenging idolatry and injustice come out of a common and deep human love for others and human love for God. This is the centrality of the Christian message and the final interpretation of God's central characteristic: God liberates because he is a Liberator and God is a Liberator because he is love and loves all human beings regardless of their differences. Any other interpretation requires a leap into the falseness of theological thinking and the manipulation of structures or rules for human benefit. Here is where I return to the basis of any hermeneutics, to the role assigned to Hermes who had to go to the gods and listen and later had to bring the message to others, thus interpreting what he had heard in his own way. Theological thinking as theological action comes out of the same process of listening and interpreting messages, messages which may not be clear and may be offered through different means of communication. Among those ways of divine communication, I would like to explore the interpretation of bones because Rwandans chose not to bury all the victims of the genocide and today a visitor is guided through churches, schools and hospitals where the bones of the dead are still present. This is a shocking reality, and the atmosphere becomes unbearable for most visitors not used to dealing with death in our contemporary society.

The unburied bones constitute a reminder of the great tragedy of the genocide. However, the bones belong to people known to those who live in the villages who daily return to visit their loved ones and to talk about their own journeys, their own hopes and their own pains. Thus, the Senegalese novelist Diop has described the daily practices of people who visit the remains of their still unburied relatives as follows:

> Loneliness was also the young woman in black who came almost every day to the polytechnic. She knew exactly which of all the tangled skeletons lying on the cold concrete were those of her little girl and her husband. She would go straight to one of the sixty-four doors of Murambi and stand in the middle of the room before two intertwined corpses: a man clutching a decapitated child against him. The young woman prayed in silence, and then left.[19]

This is not unusual and I have previously examined this phenomenon in the case of the arrested and disappeared prisoners during the regime of General Augusto Pinochet (1973–90). The number of the disappeared in Chile estimated as over 1,000 was smaller than in Argentina and certainly than in Rwanda but once the relatives of those killed found their bodies their reaction was the same: they expressed their sorrow in acts of love, they talked to the dead skulls, they touched the bones and they expressed their sentiments of deep affection and of a continuous journey together. In the case of the Chilean medical doctor Eduardo 'Coco' Paredes, arrested at La Moneda Palace on the day of the military coup (11 September 1973), his Swedish widow Eva Ahlgren and their children Raymundo and Nicolás only found out the whereabouts of his bones in 1995.[20] Paredes' remains had been found in 1991 and the Chilean forensic team using DNA and other forensic techniques had identified the remains only years later together with those of others who had been arrested and killed in September 1973. As the circumstances of his death were explained to Eva and the children by the forensic anthropologist in charge of the identification of human remains at the Santiago morgue, Paredes' widow lifted the skull in a loving manner and said 'Dear Coco, soon we will be together, very soon!'[21] When she was asked by the forensic expert if they wanted to put something in the coffin before it was sealed for burial they decided to include a bit of hair of each member of the family linked by a silken string.[22] As in many other cases, it was clear that in the case of Paredes and his family the bones still represented the loved one for his family and the family felt his presence with them 22 years after his tragic assassination.

It is my suggestion that, in the case of Rwanda or Chile or any other case, bones have a materiality that makes them texts of social reality but also theological texts in which the same image of the crucified can be found. As the symbol of the cross represents suffering as well as life for others, the unburied bones of Rwanda represent the mystery of the God who accompanies the victims and later embraces the guilt, pardon, forgiveness and reconciliation of victims and killers. Nevertheless, such liberation of the poor and the oppressed is attained at the price of a huge human cost and the questions and answers of such hermeneutics and of the theology of the liberated and the oppressed lies not at the cross but at the empty tomb. It is in that emptiness and silence of friend, God and Saviour that the women, the disciples and the people of Rwanda later found meaning and found a process of liberation from death, fear and oppression. It is to the empty tomb that I return in exploring issues of history, liberation, theologies of liberation, periphery and hermeneutics. This work maintains that liberation theology provides a praxis and a hermeneutics from the point of view of the poor and the oppressed even after the atrocities committed during the Rwandan genocide. It argues that this praxis is meaningful even after a period in which for most Rwandans it seemed that God was silent, powerless and sometimes dead.

In his manifesto about liberation theology, Iván Petrella correctly argued that the loss of 'the construction of historical projects' was one of the causes of the near-death-experience of liberation theology after the fall of the Berlin Wall.[23] Following on from that observation, I argue that a fresh 'historical project' arises out of the brutality of Rwanda in which the silence of the victims and the silence of God becomes a new marker of theological solidarity with the poor and the marginalized of the world. It is the voice of the bones of Rwanda and of the suffering God in Rwanda that becomes anew in the suffering of Darfur, of Tibet, of Latin American slums and of the thousands of victims of the humanly constructed divine killer in Iraq or Afghanistan. In all those places God speaks to his people, maybe less and less through preachers, more and more through bones.

Notes

1 Jung Mo Sung, 2007, *Desire, Market and Religion*, London: SCM Press, p. 1.

2 See José Míguez Bonino, 1975, *Revolutionary Theology Comes of Age*, London: SPCK and 1976, *Christians and Marxists: The Mutual Challenge to Revolution*, London: Hodder & Stoughton; and Guillermo Hansen (ed.), 2004, *El silbo ecuménico del espiritu: Homenaje a José Míguez Bonino en sus 80 años*, Buenos Aires: Instituto Universitario ISEDET. For a full overview of his life and work see Mario I. Aguilar, 2007, *The History and Politics of Latin American Theology*, vol. 1, *The Problem of Theological Generations* London: SCM Press, pp. 56–71.

3 On the complex understanding of orthopraxis rather than orthodoxy, see Franz J. Hinkelammert, 1997, 'Liberation Theology in the Economic and Social Context of Latin America: Economy and Theology, or the Irrationality of the Rationalized', in David Batstone, Eduardo Mendieta, Lois Ann Lorenzen and Dwight N. Hopkins (eds), *Liberation Theologies, Postmodernity and the Americas*, London and New York: Routledge, pp. 25–52.

4 See Mario I. Aguilar, 2007–8, *The History and Politics of Latin American Theology*, 3 vols, London: SCM Press.

5 See Iván Petrella, 2007, 'Theology and Liberation: Juan Luis Segundo and Three Takes on Secular Inventiveness', in Marcella Althaus-Reid, Iván Petrella and Luiz Carlos Susin (eds), *Another Possible World*, London: SCM Press, pp. 162–77.

6 Rosemary Radford Ruether, 1999, 'The Holocaust: Theological and

Ethical Reflections', in Gregory Baum (ed.), *The Twentieth Century: A Theological Overview*, Maryknoll, NY: Orbis, Ottawa: Novalis and London: Geoffrey Chapman, pp. 76–90 at p. 88.

7 The initial figure given by Philip Gaillard, head of the International Committee of the Red Cross, after the genocide was 800,000. However, over the years, many more bodies have been found and buried. Thus, the latest figure is given in John Rucyahana with James Riordan, 2007, *The Bishop of Rwanda: Finding Forgiveness Amidst a Pile of Bones*, Nashville, TN: Thomas Nelson.

8 Over the past few years Jean Hatzfeld has interviewed jailed killers and victims of the 1994 genocide, particularly in the District of Nyamata, south of the Rwandese capital Kigali, and for the first time there are testimonies in which killers and victims reflect on their own sentiments about the genocide and about God during the genocide. For a section of interviews and opinions about God during the genocide see Jean Hatzfeld, 2005, *A Time for Machetes: The Rwandan Genocide – The Killers Speak*, New York: Farrar, Straus and Giroux and London: Serpent's Tail, pp. 132–9; Jean Hatzfeld, 2005, *Into the Quick of Life: The Rwandan Genocide – The Survivors Speak*, London: Serpent's Tail.

9 Hatzfeld, *A Time for Machetes*, p. 135.

10 Hatzfeld, *A Time for Machetes*, p. 134.

11 Sung, *Desire, Market and Religion*, p. 18.

12 Mary Grey, 2007, *To Rwanda and Back: Liberation Spirituality and Reconciliation*, London: Darton, Longman and Todd.

13 Mario I. Aguilar, 1998, *The Rwanda Genocide and the Call to Deepen Christianity in Africa*, Eldoret, Kenya: AMECEA Gaba Publications, p. 90.

14 Mario I. Aguilar, 2008, *The History and Politics of Latin American Theology*, vol. 3, *A Theology of the Periphery*, London: SCM Press.

15 Grey, *To Rwanda and Back*, p. 196.

16 For a larger discussion on the possible failures by liberation theology in using Marx as a tool of social analysis for religion, see Alistair Kee, 1990, *Marx and the Failure of Liberation Theology*, London: SCM Press.

17 See Denys Turner, 1999, 'Marxism, Liberation Theology and the Way of Negation', in Christopher Rowland (ed.), *The Cambridge Companion to Liberation Theology*, Cambridge: Cambridge University Press, pp. 199–217 and his 1995 monograph on Christian mysticism, *The Darkness of God*, Cambridge: Cambridge University Press.

18 Santiago Zabala (ed.), 2005, *The Future of Religion: Richard Rorty and Gianni Vattimo*, New York: Columbia University Press, p. 54.

19 Boubacar Boris Diop, 2006, *Murambi, The Book of Bones: A Novel*, Bloomington and Indianapolis: Indiana University Press, pp. 176–7.

20 I explore his life and the legal files related to his death and disappearance in Mario I. Aguilar, 2008, *A Social History of the Catholic Church in Chile*, vol. 4, *Torture and Forced Disappearance 1973–1980*, Lewiston, NY, Queenston, Ontario and Lampeter, Wales: Edwin Mellen Press.

21 Raymundo Paredes Ahlgren, 2002, *Cuantas veces se puede matar a un hombre*, Santiago: Ediciones B Grupo Z, p. 164.

22 Ahlgren, *Cuantas veces se puede matar a un hombre*, p. 169.

23 Iván Petrella, 2007, *The Future of Liberation Theology: An Argument and Manifesto*, London: SCM Press, p. 146.

I

Rwanda and the Collapse of Theology

At the start of his theological reflection after Vatican II, Gustavo Gutiérrez emphasized the possibility of a Christian liberation from oppression and suffering that was in the hands of the Christian communities.[1] The strong reaction of liberation theology to the possibility of a heaven to come in which the poor were to find eternal consolation came about because of the fact that those who supported unjust structures in society had overemphasized that understanding of God and salvation.[2] The whole development of biblical hermeneutics and of the 'historical Jesus' debate triggered a new wave of understanding and reading of the Gospels that was to challenge the established colonial and post-colonial order, usually Christian, and its orderly parameters of established orders as given by God, including the possibility of fixed social classes and the preference of God for pious elites.[3] Thus, Jon Sobrino pointed to the importance of the Reign of God and, among its characteristics, to the theological possibility that 'the premise of the way of the praxis of Jesus is that what Jesus did will shed light on what the Reign of God is'.[4] Gutiérrez pointed to a God of Life that wanted people to be free, happy and in community. In Gutiérrez's words, 'God liberates because God is the God of life' and 'God acts in history to set the people free'.[5]

The narrative of God's acts of salvation in the Old and New Testaments continues through an ongoing history of salvation in which God's actions are delivered through the Church and within the twentieth century through the Christian communities, groups that converge with the poor, with popular culture and with popular movements.[6] God acts through the Christian communities and is alive within contemporary society because God acts in history and through theologically perceived historical projects.[7] In the words of Jung Mo Sung, 'the concept of historical subject has its roots in the Judeo-Christian tradition, which developed a notion of God as the subject of history, that is, of a God who stands outside history, and outside the world, yet directs or determines history'.[8] The communities that share the Word of God and the breaking of bread are not only the sign of the Kingdom of God to come and 'here' but 'not yet'; they represent the welcoming of God to all peoples in a way that resembles the narratives of the first Christian communities after Pentecost in the Acts of the Apostles.[9] In Gutiérrez's words, 'human beings believe in God in the context of a particular historical situation; after all, believers have their place in a cultural and social fabric'.[10] Gutiérrez's later work examined the Scriptures, accepted by Christians universally, and concluded that the poor and the marginalized, the suffering of this world and the majority still celebrate liberation and hope in a God who is with them.[11] That proclamation not only shapes their lives and their actions but expresses the Christian message through their actions, not through the statement of a high theology that via intellectual expressions convinces others to love God and neighbour so that 'there is only one history, and God is present, revealed, and saving in this single history'.[12]

If, in the case of Latin America, the Christian communities challenged the possibilities of oppression and social injustice with the Christian message, the communities of Rwanda failed to do so. In that failure one must include historical factors such as a highly organized social system that, centralized in local authorities, made it possible for an obedient and trusting mass of people (who some would say didn't have the possibility of challenging the orders of the authorities) to kill and to exterminate other people considered not to be human beings.

In this chapter, I examine the failure of a high Rwandan theology, of a triumphant Rwandan Church and of Rwandan Christians in general using the language and the analysis provided by liberation theology with the utmost hope that Christianity in Rwanda can be restored in its ritual and sociopolitical practices and that strong Christian communities in Rwanda will make the difference in the future when political systems or different ideologies collide with each other once again.

Failures in general and human failures in particular point to the possibilities of a history of salvation and a human history that come together. For it is human history that provides the possibility of God's intervention on behalf of the poor and the marginalized and it is in human history that God accompanies those who put their trust in the divine solidarity of silence, of compliance and of protest against those who have the upper voice and the structures to sustain that voice of power, status and prestige. In the words of Ignacio Ellacuría SJ, himself a martyr of history, 'salvation history is a salvation in history' because 'in fact, that historical revelation was attained historically as an interpretation of historical reality itself'.[13] Moments of human suffering in history become moments of grace as the moment of Jesus' crucifixion becomes a salvific event when it is re-read within God's action and God's plan. That moment is a human failure in which a wandering teacher and healer is crushed by the religious and political authorities but it becomes a salvific moment in history because it shows the way of the disciple who gives, in a historical context, his life for others. It is that particular utopian self-given relation with others that unites the theological affirmation of Jesus' life by Christian communities with others in the world that have given up their own historical comforts and ways of life for others in order to give witness to divine realities within human history. For example, Mohandas K. Gandhi expressed that reality within his life by dying to himself in order to unite others in peace and solidarity following his own theological understanding of history: 'Joy lies in the fight, in the attempt, in the suffering involved, not in the victory itself'.[14]

A theological negation of power and status becomes the ultimate challenge to Rome and to subsequent and contemporary empires: the negation of appearances and the possibility that history has either no meaning or a single meaning within situations of suffering, defeat and death. Jesus, raised by his Father, remains alive in his disciples after the discovery of the empty tomb. Jon Sobrino's assessment of Jesus' death provides a conclusive statement of a theological reading of history when he argues that:

> Jesus' death was not a mistake. It was the consequence of his life and this in turn was the consequence of his particular incarnation – in an anti-Kingdom which brings death – to defend its victims. If nothing more had happened after his death, if faith in Jesus had not arisen after his resurrection, his end would have been recorded in history like that of so many others.[15]

The theological reading of history provides a hermeneutical principle of divine and human closeness that does not change the nature of God but allows us to attempt to understand the possibilities and impossibilities of human behaviour in relation to divine behaviour as understood within the biblical text and the subsequent Christian canons of communal agreement. A theological reading of history in Rwanda attempted in this chapter outlines immediately the failures of human history in relation to salvation history preparing a possible theological reading of the genocide that allows hope for liberation within the following chapters.

The hope lies not solely in the possible signs of reconciliation and the implementation of new beginnings but in the possibility of suggesting that a theological reading of history, of human misery and violence takes precedence over high theologies in some of our contemporary texts and thoughts. For example, in her latest book, a moving tribute to her experience of a visit to Rwanda, Mary Grey makes two assumptions that a theology of liberation needs to underemphasize in order to provide a theological path that remains Gutiérrez's path of theology as 'a second step'. She writes at the start of her book: 'I pretend no expertise in an area where so many have suffered and others have witnessed as peace activists and conflict-resolution professionals all their lives'.[16] And she writes at the end of the book: 'But the grace of differentiation emanates from the Trinitarian economy, offering itself as the very ground of communion, a communion that respects the boundaries of difference, and as the enhancement of an identity grounded in creation in the image of God'.[17]

A theology of liberation without history denies the importance of the subject of theology; thus, a theology that liberates provides a narrative about God who can be found within the messy lives of human beings. As a result, a certain expertise in history is of the essence for theological reading. The reading of history becomes a theological tool rather than somebody else's expertise and a reading of history is used in order to avoid the application of a philosophical systematic theology on context as if the context were to be an example of a forthcoming universalism. I do not intend any kind of polemic with well-respected theologians such as Mary Grey but the grounds of communion and difference within the Trinity are very far from the developing theology of liberation and reconciliation. Such theology arises from the reflection of post-genocidal communities in Rwanda (or anywhere else where neighbours killed neighbours and they have to live with each other after the period of conflict has ended). The subject of the Trinity is one of the most complex ones for any theologian and while most Christians in Rwanda believed in the Trinity this did not make any difference to the killings of Christians by fellow Christians praising God in the same churches and in the same parishes.

It is my suggestion that a hermeneutical empathy only comes through a close examination of history in order to see the liberation by God even in the midst of historical crises and human hate of any kind. History and the construction of a post-genocidal nation state in Rwanda are categories that are interrelated (if not epistemologically at least hermeneutically) so, as Maldonado-Torres has consistently argued, 'the theology of liberation asserts theological difference from the space of enunciation of the colonial difference'.[18]

In the following sections, I outline some of the historical crises in

Rwanda during colonial and post-colonial times in order to argue that it was the model of church and the way of theologizing that led to the genocide. In my opinion, a possible way of providing a theological understanding of the past, the present and the future is to read the signs of the times and to provide encouragement to all to live their history within a fearless involvement in the reconstruction of social memories through a Christian theology and political practice that avoids the dichotomy between contemplation and political activity.[19]

The Genocidal Theological Negation

During colonial times and until 1959, the Belgian colonial power created an artificial division between Tutsis and Hutus, describing them as different from each other in physical terms.[20] For the Belgians, despite the fact that Hutus and Tutsis had intermarried for centuries, the Tutsis were tall and gracious people with smaller noses; people who in the eyes of the Belgians conducted themselves well, kept cattle and had an understanding of monarchical institutions. Thus for the Belgians, the Tutsis were closer than the Hutus to the Belgian monarchy and throughout the colonial period were preferred for education, the civil service and even the service of the Church. Rwanda became the only African country where most of the population became part of a colonial system in which Catholicism was the mark of a high social status under a God-given king of the Belgians. Indigenous religious practices were crushed and the indigenous ruler, the *mwami*, was quickly replaced by a Belgian appointed ruler with the same title.

The Tutsi cattle herders arrived in today's Rwanda by the thirteenth century from south-west Ethiopia as a dispersal group from Cushitic-speaking peoples. The Hutu also moved into Rwanda and both groups, Tutsi and Hutu, displaced the Twa hunters and gatherers who had initially populated Rwanda. The Tutsi took charge of central Rwanda and became known for their cattle, establishing a centralized kingdom dominated by an aristocracy who had cattle. This aristocracy incorporated other Tutsi who did not have cattle and also some Hutu in a patron–client relationship. Therefore the term Tutsi became associated with those who had cattle or had access to cattle while Hutu were those who worked the land or had connections with agriculture.

When, after the First World War, the Germans lost their African territories, the Urundi region formed by today's Rwanda and Burundi became part of the African Belgian territories.[21] It was easy for the Belgians to maintain what was already a centralized kingdom in

Rwanda, but labels such as Hutu and Tutsi, previously quite flexible categories, became fixed ethnic categories that allowed discrimination to arise. Racial categories made social and ethnic unrest possible. Further, the Belgians reinforced a monarchical structure that had previously been fluid. For example, since the fifteenth century the kingdoms of Rwanda revolved around the *mwami* or *umuhinza*, a Hutu priest-king, who was a *primus inter pares*; with the arrival of the Belgians, the *mwami* became a higher authority.[22] It was clear that the Belgians associated the *mwami* with their own king Leopold II and could not allow the existence of self-ruling smaller African kingdoms. Instead, the Belgians introduced self-contained communes (boroughs) which traded with one another. Within those communes the old aristocracy owned cattle; the Hutu or Tutsi did not own cattle because of their ethnic origin.[23]

By 1931, the Belgians had appointed Mutara III, the son of the first *mwami* they recognized, Yuhi V, as the only *mwami*. Mutara III died on 25 July 1959 and as he had no son a constitutional problem arose. During the discussions about a possible successor, the Hutu started asking for a republic and violence escalated. By 1959, the first attempts to kill the Tutsi population took place, at the hands of those who resented the association of the Tutsis with the Belgian colonial power. Violence and ethnic tension increased.[24] Finally, the Belgians granted independence to Rwanda on 1 July 1962. By December 1963, there were large-scale massacres of Tutsis, more than 20,000 of whom were killed.

It was in 1959 that thousands of Tutsis for the first time fled Rwanda to neighbouring countries in order to save their lives and those of their children. Paul Kagame, a two-year-old child, was in one of those fleeing vehicles, and after ending up in Uganda became the leader of the Rwandan Patriotic Front (RPF), a paramilitary group that pushed into Rwanda in 1994 and stopped the genocide by pushing the Hutu militia into the neighbouring Democratic Republic of Congo (previously Zaire). Later, Kagame became head of the RPF, vice-president and subsequently president of Rwanda.[25]

It is significant to add to this brief historical assessment of Rwanda that on 6 April 1994, the plane of Rwanda's president was shot down as it approached Kigali and a well-prepared genocide of Tutsis, Hutu moderates and those who protected Tutsis began. The killings lasted for three months until the Rwandan Patriotic Front advanced on Kigali and the Hutu government fled. It is a fact that one million people were killed by fellow citizens and that militia organized the killings by pushing Hutu 'nationalism' and by creating the daily conditions of group solidarity in which Hutus went for 'a hunt' and the prey were Tutsis who were in hiding.[26] The killing was systematic and most of the victims were killed inside churches, schools, hospitals and buildings used for community purposes. One could say that they represented the old colonial administration.

Most writers and commentators have pointed to the fact that most of the killers and the victims lived side by side in the same neighbourhoods and villages and that most of them knew each other. They were for the most part Christians, a majority of them Catholics, yet their religious obligations did not prevent them from killing others day by day. Indeed some of the killers had spoken about the fact that because they were busy with 'the hunt' they didn't have time to go to church; religious services were suspended because people were either hunting or being hunted. In the words of Theodore Nyilinkwaya, 'Everyone was called to hunt the enemy'.[27] Pio, a killer awaiting trial, explained 'the hunt' in a fuller way:

> We no longer saw a human being when we turned up a Tutsi in the swamps. I mean a person like us, sharing similar thoughts and feelings. The hunt was savage, the hunters were savage, the prey was savage – savagery took over the mind.[28]

The foreign missionaries working in Rwanda fled as soon as the killings started, most of the Rwandan bishops remained silent and some explained to foreign journalists that what was happening in Rwanda was done with the best possible intentions in order to create a better nation.

Colonial Theological Challenges

Throughout the colonial period a very stratified sense of human worthiness and dignity was implemented within a sociopolitical context in which the King of the Belgians had taken upon himself the divine mandate to evangelize through a period of colonization in which the missionary, the soldier and the colonial administrator went side by side. As V.Y. Mudimbe has argued, the *terra nullius*, the dark and empty continent of Africa, was being filled with order and with God. Within that colonization process missionaries educated indigenous populations, including Mudimbe, in the arts and humanities of European thought and in the means and ways of approaching God through Catholicism and the Catholic Church. Thus, colonialism was like a science; a well-developed ideology in itself.[29] The missionary, according to Mudimbe's analysis, 'served as an agent of a political empire, a representative of civilization, and an envoy of God'.[30] Because the missionary was responsible for the deeds of the colonial empire, the Africans had no other choice but to embrace Christianity. As the religion of the Belgian empire, it gave entry into a European social structure that was more powerful than their own indigenous religious traditions.

African groups were reorganized and a social structure of unequals was created. The monarchical system was not a democratic and egalitarian institution; Belgians were at the top of society, Tutsis in the middle and Hutus at the bottom. Enough has been written about the colonial and missionary enterprise to show that this is not today's reality. However, the social order imposed by European colonial powers could not be removed solely by providing independence, and the birth of new nations saw enormous conflict and social unrest. Oppressed groups started pushing for their rights and challenging a structure that was ethnically European and in which the Christian God was perceived as a European God.

Commentators have missed the fact that in Rwanda, with its Catholic majority, and in neighbouring Zaire (today the Democratic Republic of Congo) African theologians had questioned the established order and the European high theology. The European God had denied them equality, and the emerging African theologies provided for a universal God that was as much African as European.[31] Towards the end of the Belgian and French colonial periods, groups of African priests had asked questions about the possibility of a different way of being Christians, a different way of understanding God and the possibility of developing an African theology as well as an African indigenous Christianity. With an educated African clergy already in existence in theological centres such as Zaire and Rwanda, African priests asked questions about the canons of priestly formations in African seminaries as well as about the validity of an African Christianity that was a copy of a Belgian or a French Christianity.[32]

The development of local theologies and local Christianities permitted by Vatican II enriched the priestly formation and the liturgical development of African liturgies.[33] For example, a Zairian rite was developed without questioning the function of Christianity in maintaining social inequality within Rwanda that denied the existence or action of a liberating God within a newly independent Africa.[34] Christian communities continued growing in numbers but the shortage of priests and catechists meant that large numbers did not receive the necessary Christian instruction that could make a difference to a stratified system of inequality that resembled colonial times in which the Catholic Church and Catholic bishops were not able to influence their Catholic elites. Those elites in Rwanda were already preparing paramilitary groups in order to effectively create the conditions for an ethnic cleansing that in the case of Rwanda became a full genocide of the Tutsi.

Genocidal Challenges

The inability to provide a theology of solidarity, hope and cooperation between different groups in Rwanda provided a reminder that in Africa blood was thicker than water: family, kin and ethnic groups were more powerful than membership of a community based on Christian baptism and the use of water in order to dissolve the divisions created by ethnicity and social identity.

On 6 April 1994, President Juvenal Habyarimama was returning from Tanzania where he had attended peace talks in order to secure a ceasefire between different warring factions in Rwanda. At 8.30 p.m., as his plane approached Kanombe military base in Kigali, three missiles were fired at the presidential plane. The plane crashed in the grounds of the presidential palace and all on board died: President Habyarimama, the newly elected Burundian President Cyprien Ntaryamira, Rwanda's Chief of Staff Deogratias Nsabimana, several senior members of the presidential staff and members of the French crew that operated the plane. The Rwandan government blamed the Rwandan Patriotic Front for killing the Hutu president while other Rwandan diplomats blamed the Belgians for firing the missiles. It was clear though that whoever had fired the missiles had access to the military base. The Rwandan government was immediately taken by Hutu extremists who mobilized the militia in order to exercise violent retaliation against the Tutsi population.

Years later, it is possible to assert as a fact that the genocide had already been planned; lists of Hutu moderates, enemies of the government and the Tutsi leadership in Kigali were already in circulation. The media frenzy orchestrated by the militia called upon all Hutus to defend the Hutu government and to attack the Tutsis. The massacres in Kigali started on 7 April 1994 and spread throughout the country as groups of militia were sent to different districts to coordinate the killings with government personnel. The possibility of escape was very small as Rwanda remains a country locked in hills and with inadequate means of transport. Those who escaped the first killings were those who owned means of transport; then, as roadblocks were placed all over the country, they were those who managed to escape to the swamps and forests and were not discovered by the militia. As usual, the poor had no way of escaping while those who had some means were able to escape or were able to bribe others in order to survive.

The most shocking stories of the genocide related to a common phenomenon: that of awaiting one's death without hope of anything else. Those who gathered in churches and schools or hills around their villages awaited their own death with the arrival of the militia. Philip Gourevitch collected the story of seven Tutsi pastors who, on 16 April 1994, wrote to their Adventist leader Pastor Elizaphan Ntakirutimana requesting he had a word with the local governor because they feared that on the next day they were going to be killed at Mugonero Adventist Centre and at the hospital.[35] The pastors ended the letter in the following religious manner: 'We believe that, with the help of God who entrusted you the leadership of this flock, which is going to be destroyed, your intervention will be highly appreciated, the same way as the Jews were saved by Esther.'[36] According to Ntakirutimana he wrote back to them saying that nothing could be done and neither he nor the governor could intervene. After the massacre of thousands of Tutsis in Mugonero he asserted his innocence, but in 1996 the FBI arrested him in Laredo, Texas, accusing him of leading and organizing the killings of the Tutsi population to whom he ministered.

The killing was systematic and predictable. Lists were circulated before the arrival of the militia while people were being encouraged to congregate in public spaces in order to escape the violence. The militia gathered Hutu males in football fields and open spaces and briefed them on the job to be done. They searched for and killed those who were hiding from morning to late afternoon and later they drank and feasted together until returning to their homes, their wives and their children. It is very striking that the killings and their organization were for the most part public, unlike other conflicts in which a state apparatus created private spaces outside the view and the rules of a nation in order to torture and kill, as in the case of South Africa or Chile.

The foreign missionaries were passive and left, following orders to evacuate their own embassies, a pattern unheard of in other situations. The colonial ordering had been well developed even within independence and the killings were possible because the colonial world was still present within the government, the churches and the people. The international community failed to intervene and the poor and the marginalized of Rwanda were left on their own to deal with killers who were finally in control of a process of disordering the colonial and Christian world that they considered 'the past'.[37] Thus, Rwanda became a killing field very similar to those of Latin America in which Christians tortured and killed in the name of a project of ordering, while those killed and tortured were also part of the same symbolic community of God and Church divided by a different understanding of Christianity, nationalism and patriotism.

Within the violence that reigned in communal terrors and the nightmares of the frenzy of evil that took over the land I would like to dwell on one of the first killings in Kigali. It is no coincidence that one of the first killings took place at the Jesuit retreat centre in Kigali.[38] Those who were at the centre of any possible resistance had to be annihilated first; thus, at 7 a.m. on 7 April 1994, seventeen people were killed at the Christus Centre in Kigali. The group included priests, seminarians, lay people and staff. An hour after the radio announcement that the Rwandese president had been assassinated members of the Presidential Guard arrived at the retreat centre. They asked to see everybody's ID cards, but nobody had them because they didn't need them at that time when they were praying in the chapel. Ten minutes later the armed guards separated the Rwandese from the Europeans and locked them in different rooms. Among the expatriates there were three Belgian Jesuits, and three Spanish women who belonged to the lay organization Vita et Pax who were kept in the dining room. When they were released at 2.20 p.m. they found seventeen bodies in the room where the Rwandese had been locked. Two of them, a young woman and a diocesan priest, had been spared. However, among the victims there were eight members of Vita et Pax, four diocesan priests, a social worker, a cook and three Jesuits.

One must ask why the Presidential Guard targeted the retreat centre. The African Rights Report argues very convincingly that during February 1994 the retreat centre had been a place of refuge for Tutsi refugees and that the Jesuits had denied a request by the authorities to expel the refugees from the retreat centre. It is possible, the report argues, that those who were killed were assumed to be refugees. However, it is clear that priests at the retreat centre had formed an association, 'Patrie', to defend the rights of refugees.[39]

The killing of the Jesuits in Kigali resembles those of other Jesuits in time of conflict within other nations such as El Salvador where the whole community of the Jesuits working at the university were killed, including Ignacio Ellacuría SJ, because of their involvement in public life trying to diffuse conflict through direct mediation between the guerrillas and the state.[40] In the case of Rwanda, those three Jesuits to be killed first symbolized the full extent of the genocide that was unfolding. Two of them were Tutsi, Chrysologue Mahame (67) and

Patrick Gahizi (48), but one of them was a Hutu, Innocent Rutagambwa (46), who had been working at the Jesuit provincial office from 1990 to February 1994 and had translated the *Spiritual Exercises* of Ignatius of Loyola into Kinyarwanda.[41] A portrait of the three Jesuits would explain the fact that the Presidential Guard executed first the Jesuits, then those Hutu leaders opposed to the genocide and the Tutsi leadership in Kigali.

Fr Mahame was the long-time Superior at the Christus Centre having been the first Rwandese Jesuit. Born in Kibeho he had joined the Jesuits in 1952 in Dujuma, Zaire. He studied theology at Eagenhoven in Belgium and was ordained as a priest in 1961 taking his final vows in 1970. In 1992, he helped the creation of the human rights organization Association des Volontaires de la Paix (AVP), an association of which he was the legal representative having participated many times in mediation between the government and the RPF. He had had disagreements with the Rwandan president and it is possible to argue that this was the reason why the Presidential Guard of all military units was sent to the Jesuit retreat centre after the Rwandan president was killed. Fr Gahizi joined the Jesuits in Cyangugu in 1977, studied philosophy at Kimwenza in Zaire and theology at the Gregorian University in Rome. He was ordained in 1984 and continued further studies in Rome and Quebec. He took final vows in 1990 and when the war broke out he was in prison for two weeks. Later he became Provincial's delegate and superior of the scholastic residence at the University of Butare. Fr Rutagambwa entered the Jesuits in Cyangugu in 1969 and studied philosophy and theology at Kimwenza and African linguistics at the University of Lumumbashi in Zaire and continued further studies at the Gregorian University in Rome. He was ordained in 1979 and took his final vows in 1987, returning to Rwanda where he taught at the high school in Gisenyi where he was supposed to return in 1994 after his years of service at the Jesuit Provincial offices.

The killing of the Jesuits was the signal awaited by others to start the systematic killings. Within the post-independence life of Rwandans, the Jesuits had brought their own Jesuit spirituality and had aimed at shaping the Rwandan leadership with a Christian spirituality of contemplation and action following in the steps of Ignatius of Loyola.[42] They were dangerous for the Hutu extremists because they could have organized a resistance to the killings. Therefore, in a strange manner, the first to be killed were not Tutsi politicians or Hutu moderates but those who were praying and searching for God at a retreat centre. Once those spiritual masters were out of the way the large-scale killing began.

Once the city of Kigali had been secured and the international observers kept out of Rwanda, the militia mobilized its members to rural Rwanda and the killing started village by village, church by church, neighbourhood by neighbourhood. According to the 1991 Rwandan census Kibuye had the highest concentration of Tutsis within Rwanda. They numbered 252,000 before the genocide. By the end of 1994 there were only 7,000 to 8,000 Tutsis alive in Kibuye. Kibuye is only one of the many examples of a systematic extermination of an ethnic group by fellow nationals and fellow Christians within Rwanda. The killings were well planned and directed by the Prefect of Kibuye, Clément Kayishema, a medical doctor.[43] He redirected some of the frightened Tutsis to so-called 'safe areas' such as Kibuye parish, Gatwaro Stadium and Kibuye Hospital. After a couple of weeks attacks started on those gathered within the 'safe areas' with reinforcements arriving from Gisenyi, Ruhengeri and Cyangugu, where massive killings had already taken place. The killings had already started on 7 April 1994, when those who could not run to the hills, mainly the elderly, were massacred by militia. The majority of the Tutsis sought shelter on the hills where their parents had already sought refuge during the ethnic attacks on Tutsis in 1973. After days fighting the militia, the Tutsi who were on the hills were forced to flee to the commune office in Mabanza and from there were directed to Kibuye town, a seven-hour walk.

The massacres in Kibuye started on 9 and 10 April 1994 when the European sisters at Mubuga were instructed to leave in a vehicle provided by the Prefect, leaving the Tutsi refugees defenceless. On 17 April 1994, soldiers mounted guns and started shooting into the crowded Gatwaro Stadium from 1 to 8 p.m. Grenades were thrown in, and people with machetes slaughtered anybody who tried to escape. A few managed to escape due to the exhaustion of the militia but were systematically tracked down in the countryside and hacked to death.

Another public massacre took place at Kibuye parish. Children, old men and women were brought to the parish compound; according to a census carried out on 15 April 1994 by Fr Boniface Senyenzi and a Belgian woman there were 7,200 refugees at the parish. The place was crowded with people staying in the courtyard of the church, the St Jean Home, the school and all the areas close to the church. When a French officer, Lt Col. Eric de Stabenrath, found the remnants of the killings at Kibuye parish he counted 4,300 bodies piled one on top of another. According to survivors the militia arrived by boat and killed young Tutsi first, searching house by house. On 16 April 1994, 200 Twa attacked the refugees at the parish compound but were repelled. However, on the following day, Sunday 17 April 1994, some 450 men, including soldiers, policemen and prison wardens, plus 400 members of the militia, attacked the parish refugees who sought refuge inside the church building. They killed them all with grenades, machine guns and machetes. Louis Rutaganira (44), a businessman in the area before the killings, described the horror as follows:

> There were so many people dead. But the killers wanted to single out the survivors. So they threw tear-gas inside the church which forced the living to get up. Immediately those with machetes came in to finish off the living. Those who managed to run outside were macheted on the doorstep. Those of us who survived were the ones hidden under dead bodies. The finishing off lasted from 3.00 to 5.00 pm. We were choking with the tear-gas. But we were so buried by dead bodies that it was difficult to get up even if we wanted to.[44]

The St Jean Home was also attacked and five priests including Abbé Gahinda, who had come from Nyundo, as well as 200 other people, were killed. The killers departed by 7 p.m. as darkness approached, leaving more or less everybody dead apart from a few who had taken refuge on the roof of the Catholic mission. The massacres stopped with the arrival of French soldiers who were stationed at the Ecole Technique Normale and on 30 April, two weeks after the massacres, only 60 frightened survivors left the pile of bodies. They were helped by other locals who organized boats that took them to Ijwi Island in Zaire.

The area of Kibuye became a catalyst of a larger story. Victims were betrayed by neighbours and friends and a number of clergy failed to stop the genocide, though there were some priests and religious who protected the refugees until death. Thus, one of the survivors paid tribute to the mission superior, Fr Boniface Senyenzi, Fr Theophilus from Rwamatamu, five religious brothers from the Major Seminary and a Belgian nun, Tante Emma, who ran a guest house. Some Hutu brothers had warned them about the arrival of the militia and they decided to stay and organize the protection of the refugees.

The collapse of a 'high theology' meant in practice that the commandment to love God and neighbour to the end was the only central theological understanding of Christians in Rwanda at the time of the genocide. Many failed to protect the Tutsi neighbours, others gave their lives precisely obeying Christ's commandment of love and remained the presence of a liberating God within the genocide. By the time that the genocide ended in July 1994 the fields, roads, churches and hospitals of Rwanda were covered with blood and it seemed to most religious practitioners that God had abandoned Rwanda as the missionaries had left, the churches remained closed, the corpses were everywhere and the joy of the gospel was far from the land of the thousand hills.

In the following chapters, I shall examine the possible 'death of God' in Rwanda and the post-genocidal theological narratives given by members of the Christian communities themselves, those who killed and those who escaped the killings in the absence of God in Rwanda.

Notes

1 Gustavo Gutiérrez, 1973, *A Theology of Liberation: History, Politics and Salvation*, Maryknoll, NY: Orbis, and 1983, *The Power of the Poor in History*, Maryknoll, NY: Orbis.

2 Gustavo Gutiérrez, 2004, 'God's Revelation and Proclamation in History', in *The Power of the Poor in History*, Eugene, OR: Wipf & Stock, pp. 3–22, at p. 18.

3 For God's option for the poor in Luke, see Jorge Pixley and Clodovis Boff, 1989, *The Bible, the Church and the Poor: Biblical, Theological and Pastoral Aspects of the Option for the Poor*, Tunbridge Wells: Burns & Oates, pp. 58–63.

4 Jon Sobrino, 1996, 'Central Position of the Reign of God in Liberation Theology', in Jon Sobrino and Ignacio Ellacuría (eds), *Systematic Theology: Perspectives from Liberation Theology*, Maryknoll, NY: Orbis, pp. 38–74, at p. 48.

5 Gustavo Gutiérrez, 1991, *The God of Life*, London: SCM Press, p. 3.

6 Ronaldo Muñoz, 1991, *The God of Christians*, Tunbridge Wells: Burns & Oates, pp. 16–24.

7 Thus, Juan Luis Segundo consistently argued that events in history and historical projects 'are indications of the fact that history has meaning, and that it is reasonable to wager on that meaning', in 'Revelation, Faith, Signs of the Times', in Ignacio Ellacuría SJ and Jon Sobrino SJ (eds), 1993, *Mysterium Liberationis: Fundamental Concepts of Liberation Theology*, Maryknoll, NY: Orbis and North Blackburn, Victoria: Collins Dove, pp. 328–49, at p. 346.

8 Jung Mo Sung reminds us that 'our modern world replaced this notion of God as subject of history with the notion of the human being as the subject of history'. See 'The Human Being as Subject: Defending the Victims', in Iván Petrella (ed.), 2005, *Latin American Liberation Theology: The Next Generation*, Maryknoll, NY: Orbis, pp. 1–19, at p. 7.

9 Leonardo Boff, 1986, *Ecclesiogenesis: The Base Communities Reinvent the Church*, Maryknoll, NY: Orbis.

10 Gutiérrez, *The God of Life*, p. xv.

11 Gustavo Gutiérrez, 1993, 'Option for the Poor', in Ellacuría and Sobrino (eds), *Mysterium Liberationis: Fundamental Concepts of Liberation Theology*, pp. 235–50.

12 Pablo Richard, 1993, 'Theology in the Theology of Liberation', in

Ellacuría and Sobrino (eds), *Mysterium Liberationis: Fundamental Concepts of Liberation Theology*, pp. 150–68, at p. 160.

13 Ignacio Ellacuría SJ, 1976, *Freedom Made Flesh*, Maryknoll, NY: Orbis, p. 15.

14 Richard Attenborough (ed.), 2002, *Gandhi: In My Own Words*, London: Hodder & Stoughton, p. 3.

15 Jon Sobrino SJ, 1994, *Jesus the Liberator: A Historical-Theological Reading of Jesus of Nazareth*, Tunbridge Wells: Burns & Oates, p. 210.

16 Mary Grey, 2007, *To Rwanda and Back: Liberation Spirituality and Reconciliation*, London: Darton, Longman and Todd, p. viii.

17 Grey, *To Rwanda and Back*, p. 197.

18 Nelson Maldonado-Torres, 2005, 'Liberation Theology and the Search for the Lost Paradigm: From Radical Orthodoxy to Radical Diversality', in Petrella (ed.), *Latin American Liberation Theology*, pp. 39–61, at p. 46.

19 See the extension of this theological argument in Mario I. Aguilar, 2008, *Contemplation and Political Activity*, London: SPCK.

20 The smallest group, the Twa hunters and gatherers, were very small in number and never part of the public social life of colonial Rwanda.

21 For full bibliographies on the Belgian colonial period in Rwanda, see John B. Webster, 1966, 'The Political Development of Rwanda and Burundi', Occasional Paper no. 16, Maxwell Graduate School of Citizenship and Public Affairs, The Program of Eastern African Studies, Syracuse University, pp. 101–21 and Ian Linden (with Jane Linden), 1977, *Church and Revolution in Rwanda*, Manchester: Manchester University Press.

22 Ian Linden uses *mwami* in his text when referring to the Rwandan king, *umwami* when referring to the *umuhinza*-like Hutu religious leader/land priest, *Church and Revolution in Rwanda*, p. 289.

23 See Pierre Bettez Gravel, 1965, 'Life on the Manor in Gisaka (Rwanda)', *Journal of African History* 6:3, pp. 323–31.

24 This increasing tension is pointed out by Helen Rodere, an anthropologist who was conducting fieldwork in Rwanda at that time. See Helen Rodere, 1970, 'Fieldwork in Rwanda 1959–1960', in P. Golde (ed.), *Women in the Field: Anthropological Experiences*, Chicago: Aldine, pp. 149–50, at p. 162.

25 Paul Kagame was born on 23 October 1957 and moved with his family to Uganda after the killing of over 20,000 Tutsis in 1959. They stayed at the Gahunge refugee camp in Toro. In 1979, Kagame joined the National Resistance Army (NRA) led by Yoweri Museveni. In 1986, Museveni's army overthrew the government of Milton Obote and Museveni became president of Uganda. In that year Kagame, together with his close friend Fred Rwigema, formed the Rwandan Patriotic Front made up of Rwandan Tutsis who had fought in Museveni's army. In October 1990, the RPF made its first attempt to enter Rwanda and Rwigema was killed. Kagame was at that time undergoing military training in Fort Leavenworth, Kansas. A second attempt by the RPF was also crushed by Rwandan, Belgian and French forces in 1992–93; however, by 1994 the RPF took part in the Arusha accord for peace and was allowed participation in Rwandan public life. The start of the genocide halted any progress and the end of the genocide was marked by the RPF taking full control of Rwanda on 4 July 1994 and the overthrow of the self-appointed government of Jean Kambanda.

When President Bizimungu was deposed in March 2000 Kagame moved from vice-president to acting president; in 2003, he became the first democratically elected president of Rwanda after the 1994 genocide.

26 The 'hunt' as an expression by Hutu killers is used consistently in the interviews conducted by Jean Hatzfeld after the genocide. See Jean Hatzfeld, 2005, *A Time for Machetes: The Rwandan Genocide – The Killers Speak*, New York: Farrar, Straus and Giroux, and London: Serpent's Tail.

27 Philip Gourevitch, 1999, *We Wish To Inform You That Tomorrow We Will Be Killed With Our Families*, London: Picador, p. 24.

28 Hatzfeld, *A Time for Machetes*, p. 42.

29 V.Y. Mudimbe, 1994, *The Idea of Africa*, Bloomington and Indianapolis: Indiana University Press, London: James Currey, pp. 118–23; see review of the book by Mario I. Aguilar, 1996, *Africa: Journal of the International African Institute* 66:2, pp. 301–2.

30 V.Y. Mudimbe, 1988, *The Invention of Africa: Gnosis, Philosophy and the Order of Knowledge*, Bloomington and Indianapolis: Indiana University Press, London: James Currey, p. 45.

31 See a history of this theology in Aylward Shorter, 1988, *Toward a Theology of Inculturation*, London: Geoffrey Chapman.

32 Those questions came from contribution to a dossier with the title *Des prêtres noirs s'interrogent*, Paris: Présence Africaine, 1956. For a short overview of African Theology see A. Ngindu Mushete, 1994, 'An Overview of African Theology', in Rosino Gibellini (ed.), *Paths of African Theology*, London: SCM Press, pp. 9–26.

33 Within the documents of Vatican II, the idea that culture made human beings authentic and fully human was stressed, see for example *Gaudium et Spes* § 53.

34 For some developments in Christian liturgies within Africa after Vatican II, see Elochukwu E. Uzukwu, 1994, 'Inculturation and the Liturgy (Eucharist)', in Gibellini (ed.), *Paths of African Theology*, pp. 95–114.

35 Those signing the letter were Pastors Ezekiel Semugeshi, Isaka Rucondo, Seth Rwanyabuto, Eliezer Seromba, Seth Sebihe, Jerome Gakwaya and Ezekias Zigirinshuti.

36 Gourevitch, *We Wish To Inform You*, p. 42.

37 See 'The International Response to Conflict and Genocide: Lessons from the Rwanda Experience', *The Tablet*, 23 March 1996, p. 148.

38 A full report of the massacre at the Christus Centre in Kigale can be found in African Rights (1995), *Rwanda: Death, Despair and Defiance*, London: African Rights, pp. 863–5.

39 African Rights, *Rwanda: Death, Despair and Defiance*, p. 865.

40 See Mario I. Aguilar, 2008, *The History and Politics of Latin American Theology*, vol. 2, London: SCM Press, chapters 1 and 2.

41 Biographical details of these three Jesuits are available in African Rights, *Rwanda: Death, Despair and Defiance*, pp. 863–4.

42 For an outline of the history of the Jesuits and the strength of contemporary Jesuit spirituality, particularly through the Ignatian Exercises given to Christians within the growing non-Western Christianity, see Aguilar, *The History and Politics of Latin American Theology*, vol. 2, chapter 4.

43 Clément Kayishema was born in 1954 and attended the National University of Rwanda. From 1986 to 1991 he was the medical director of the hospital in Nyanza. In 1987, he married Mukandoli and they had two children. He was appointed prefect of Kibuye on 3 July 1992. On 21 May 1999, he was sentenced to life imprisonment by the International Criminal Tribunal for Rwanda (ICTR). The ICTR was created on 8 November 1994 by the United Nations Security Council in order to prosecute those responsible for crimes against humanity in Rwanda between 1 January and 31 December 1994; see UN Resolution 955. French name: *Tribunal pénal international pour le Rwanda*. Kinyarwanda name: *Urukiko Nshinjabyaha Mpuzamahanga rwagenewe u Rwanda*.

44 African Rights, *Rwanda: Death, Despair and Defiance*, p. 421.

2

A Hermeneutics of Bones

As the persecuted, the bereaved and the starving started repopulating the landscapes of Rwanda after 1994, the order of the day was to survive. The national process of reconciliation could be compared to the return of thousands of Germans to their bombarded cities and their destroyed homes after the allied invasion. There was peace and the war had ended; however, there was the silence of the empty destroyed cities as well as the cautious silence of the heart. No war is a triumph and no conflict brings a better future. On the contrary, the killing of thousands provides the possibility of empty fields, empty factories and empty minds. Indeed, it is my own experience that after a moment of great crisis, great violence and intense violence, there is no need to speak but a certain overwhelming tiredness brings the body and the mind to ordinary concerns. Thus, it is only through returning to pleasurable activities and to a certain personal and social security that human beings heal and learn once again to laugh and to love. The possibility of dealing with a failed utopia does not come immediately to mind but the heart longs for loved ones and for the warmth of friends and of family.

That human process of regeneration takes place in a similar manner for those who long for their own symbolic and ritual family and that was the case of Rwandans. After some security was established and within a period of hardship because of the emptiness of the gardens and the fields without crops they returned to their ordinary activities: they sat with others and asked about relatives and loved ones while others wandered into the church compounds wondering if a priest was going to return in order to call the community to prayer and to the celebration of the Eucharist. It sounds strange, yes, the celebration of the thanksgiving to God, at a time when for some God had deserted them while for others God would never be able to forgive their own rage, their hate and their past killings. Rwanda was a nation in silence and within that silence relatives continued visiting the places where their relatives had died and their homes where silence reigned and nobody wanted to discuss the things that happened at the 1994 genocide. The desire for food and warmth came first, the desire for God and others came second. However, the desire to understand came last and took years of national and international investigations.

After the initial composition of lists of those who had incited the genocide the Rwandan government instituted local courts that dealt with thousands of prisoners in jail who had the opportunity to confront their victims in communal occasions of a legal nature and who, provided they showed repentance, were sentenced to community service rather than periods of penal seclusion. It didn't help that subsequent Rwandan governments, and particularly that of President Paul Kagame, sought national reconciliation but avoided the possibility of a national truth and reconciliation commission as in South Africa, where the churches were very prominent as main actors within civil society in general and as close partners of the state in particular.

The Death of God

During the three months of the Rwandan genocide, churches were empty and outside the Rwandan capital Kigali they were filled with persecuted people who were eventually massacred within the churches. God seemed to have died and the killers' narratives reiterated several years later their theological understanding of a God that was represented as ethnic, either Hutu or Tutsi, with the consequence that the God of the Tutsis was dead, he didn't exist, because he didn't prevent the killing of thousands of Tutsis at the hand of the Hutu militia.

The face of God in Africa was represented for most Rwandese by the dedicated missionaries who had baptized them, taught them in their schools, cured them in their clinics and helped them to pray to a God that previously had been associated with Europeans and with the Belgian and French colonial powers. One of the striking phenomena in Rwanda 1994 was that, in contrast to other places, the foreign missionaries were quickly collected by peace-keeping personnel and shipped out of Rwanda at once. For example, Valérie Nyirarudodo, a midwife at the Sainte-Marthe Maternity Hospital in Nyamata, recalled the arrival of the UN soldiers and the flight of the European sisters: 'They pulled up in front of the gate. They told the three white sisters to pack small bags immediately. They said "No point any more in wasting time with goodbyes, right now is goodbye".'[1] The immediate reaction of the Swiss sisters was to bring with them their Rwandan colleagues. However, the soldiers had been instructed not to transport

Rwandans. As the convoy left, the militia fired their arms in jubilation as they initially feared that the European soldiers were going to fight them. Later, the African sisters were killed like all the others.

Unburied Bones

As already outlined, most of those thousands killed inside churches, hospitals and schools were not buried; their bones remain objects of curiosity for visitors and a reminder of loving relatives to their families. On a daily basis some relatives go to talk to their loved ones and the cohesion between a physical and a metaphysical world is ever strengthened. This communion between living human beings and their ancestors who live in another world is not unusual; what becomes unusual is the centrality of a hermeneutics of presence that dictates readings and interpretations of memory through silence and the memories of silence. The reality of an event of death and despair that took place at a particular space and time during the genocide becomes for a person who was left alive a place and an important place in daily life. In John Inge's analysis, 'what is undifferentiated space becomes for us significant place by virtue of our familiarity with it'.[2]

In this chapter, I attempt a theological reading of Boubacar Boris Diop's *Murambi*, followed by a reflection on bones, theology and liberation in order to suggest that in all situations of disaster the hermeneutical text of the Bible has become a secondary reading, making biblical and theological hermeneutics 'a second act' while the first theological act is the presence and empathy with the human and the divine in a place of bones. Thus, whereas Gutiérrez spoke of theology as 'a second act' this chapter proposes that hermeneutics is 'a second act', not only because it is a process of interpretation of an already past event but also because the sole principle of Christian interpretation is love. Love is the first and only central act in the active silence of God. The centrality of God's love denied by human beings through genocide becomes the only possible theology and the texts of this theology are not pages of a book but the history of humanity and of God written in each one of those precious bones. Bones are not only texts to be interpreted, but represent the presence of God among his people. In the context of genocide, that presence is silent and in the context of a post-genocidal society spaces of genocidal memories remain places of silence and encounter with God. They become places where not unlike cemeteries a physical mediation between the physical and the metaphysical world can be observed and indeed experienced.

Aesthetic Theologizing

One of the greatest possibilities of liberation theology has always been the possibility of utopia, the possibility of dreaming that a better world could eventually come because 'utopias are not illusions' but 'they are imaginative and creative, but realistic possibilities for the future'.[3] The dreamer is not imagining an outside reality. Instead, through a liberating praxis, through actions that speak of liberation here and now, the dreamer prepares a community for the realities to come, enjoying the immediacy of the Eros, of the desire for God and other human beings, rather than the desire for commodities or for material things. In this, liberation theology connects the utopian dream, and as a result the dreamer, with a historical project.[4]

In the case of genocide, the historical realities of suffering and dehumanization speak at all times of a lack of freedom and of a need for liberation. However, neither those who have suffered nor those who have not suffered the consequences of the Rwandan genocide are able to see another reality without the possibility of dreaming. Dreaming does not stop during genocide and utopian moments keep the sufferer and the victim connected to a world outside the body in a needed sense of touch, of feeling and of simplicity. For example, during General Pinochet's attempt at the extermination of all political opponents, particularly those who were actively opposing his dictatorial regime with arms, torture, violence and degrading treatments, periods of torture were aimed at destroying the person, destroying hope and destroying utopia.[5] The hooded or blindfolded prisoners waited in silence for the next kind of pain and were presumed destroyed by their torturers. However, as the prisoners of the notorious Villa Grimaldi, a prisoners' camp where torture was a daily reality, sat at the only bench that was available, they felt the warmth of others and they could smell the scent of the rosebushes beside the bench.[6] Cold bodies that were underfed dreamt again of a better world and they dreamt to see their families and their loved ones but *only* if, I repeat, *only* if they were able to face their torturers with the dignity of human beings. That dignity remained with the prisoners and the tortured if they kept the power of dreaming, a power that could not be taken away by the fragility of the body and the continual pain of beatings and electric shocks. However, the prisoners' dreams related to a common historical project of changing society and sharing the goods of the earth, rather than to personal possessions or prestige within society.

Within this experience of liberation, utopia and a historical project, according to Sheila Cassidy 'the final victory over their terror of pain and physical death is the last of a thousand victories and defeats in the war which is fought daily and hourly in the human mind and soul: the war in the overcoming of self'.[7] It is important to realize that the healing of those tortured and those in post-traumatic shock comes not from forgetting the pain and the horror but from the acceptance of it as part of a process of life. In therapies for torture survivors, art and creativity are of the essence to cope with feelings of unworthiness and of loss. In rebuilding the person as a human being loved by God and by others, aesthetic forms realize the possibility of the touch of God in healing the past by revisiting it in different forms. Poetry and writing become another form in which the broken person does not forget but takes the past as unchangeable and the future as full of promise, full of opportunities; new dreams arise in which the liberating power of the God of Life becomes for those who are members of a faith community the continuity of a human dignity that cannot be taken away, even in death.

It is with this understanding of aesthetic knowledge and of theological liberation that I read the novel *Murambi*.[8] It is a fictional piece that depicts human realities and historical facts but that allows the voiceless and powerless to regain their voice and to theologize about events of the past. In the words of Eileen Julien:

> It does what a creative and transformative work alone can do. It distils this history and gives voice to those who can no longer speak – recovering, as best we can, the full, complex lives concealed in the statistics of genocide and rendering their humanity. In thinking about the gruesome murder of hundreds of thousands of people and this book – a frail object – we confront the enormous disproportion between the work of art, as beautiful and powerful as it may be, and the terrible events it symbolizes.[9]

I have already mentioned in my assessment of Latin American theologies today that the area of 'aesthetic theologizing' has remained unexplored.[10] This lack of exploration remains even more acute within African theology because there are fewer literate people in Africa than in Latin America. Speech remains the way societies communicate, and is the accepted way of thinking theologically. Within this process of 'aesthetic theologizing' I argue that in the past few years the connections between theology and literature in Africa have not been redeveloped but certainly a great number of African writers have increased the possibilities of liberating the oppressed by rethinking utopia, particularly Christian utopia, in literature.

It is at this stage of God's life in Africa that African theology poses a contradiction. As in Lévi-Strauss's concept of 'binary oppositions', creativity arises through the opposition of terms rather than by reaffirming a familiar idea in new words. The process of theologizing is primarily oral; however, the way to progress, leadership and success in Africa is through writing and through Western education. The first step of theologizing remains within communities with little access to the commodities of the African elites; however, the way religious and social utopias can be rethought comes through a process of writing – manifestos, impossible dreams. In fact, African aesthetic theologizing is caught between the power of the spoken word and the power of the written word: it is not a coincidence that (as noted by Éloi Messi Motogo, commenting on the impact of Vatican II in Africa) 'the conciliar reforms have been most evident in the field of liturgy'.[11] The lively African liturgies and the liturgical experimentation that has included the use of traditional songs, dances and even the incorporation of caterpillars on the altar is a testimony to the creativity offered by African faith communities that have been given the chance to theologize aesthetically by incorporating beauty in the liturgy taken from their own experience and life rather than imported from Europe.

In most cases, though, African theologizing moves between the poles of a creative dichotomy that can only operate within a colonial or a neo-colonial world. In those modes of globalized existence, the oral and the written provide a place and a role within social and political structures that are created from the outside. Within a renewed mode of theological coloniality, forms and understandings remain the same everywhere, forms, shapes, colours and understandings brought by the European missionaries; within a neo-colonial system of theologizing foreign preachers and foreign corporations 'empower' Africans with the (in)dignity of the consumer or the absolute control of God by the power of an ever louder speech taught by the great US preachers of the mega-churches and the Mega-God which implies a neo-colonial project using images and understandings coming out of that Great Nation of God-fearing people north of the Great River. Within this ongoing development of foreign evangelical preachers that arrive in Africa, the consumerist dream is played once again not through the organizational possibilities of the managers of organized mega-religion but through the capabilities they have, in the words of Jung Mo Sung 'to manipulate and satisfy the consumer's desires'.[12]

For orality in any theology, be it African or otherwise, provides a framework of acceptance so that the more words that are spoken the more powerful the domination of God's narrative and God's action in the world by the one who can utter those words. It is the power of the words of Martin Luther King, who speaks to the oppressed telling them at the beginning of the campaign for civil rights that they are marching to the Promised Land; however, he becomes later the prophetic word that tells them 'I have seen the Promised Land', and he is killed!

Aesthetic theologizing and the hermeneutics of bones require neither orality nor literacy but silence. Theologizing about God through bones and genocide challenges the Western paradigm of literacy, with progress and development attached to it, and it also challenges the paradigm of orality, in which the power of speech becomes the possibility of accessing God, his thoughts and his plans. For, in both models of theologizing, empowerment is given to the mediator and to the learned while theologizing remains 'a second act', action is always the first act. If in the Latin American context actions of solidarity with the poor and the marginalized expressed the presence of God, the context of Rwanda remains a mystery encircled in the silence of bones and the possibility of understanding God's presence remains with those who are close in spirit to the reality of thousands of unburied bones in Rwanda today. Shall I call them the keepers of the bones or the custodians of God's presence? Whatever the appropriate name, there are many people in post-genocide Rwanda who live a daily existence in relation to those bones. They resemble the bereaved who must remain close to the loved one who is gone or the person in love who needs to be beside the source of that love every day and every minute. In a context in which the churches failed, the faithful Africans do not lose their faith but continue communicating their love for the members of their families, their ancestors and their companions on the road.

The God of Nyamata

Let us turn to *Murambi* and its theological narratives.[13] Diop's moving novel narrates in the first part some of the turmoil and confusion that affected Rwandans at the time of the genocide by letting some of them speak in the first person. In the case of Michel Serumundo, his reflections speak of the limited utopia that was left in Rwanda and the hope he had that yet another ethnic killing would be only a small incident rather than a full-blown national event. He articulates this as follows:

> The looting could start at any moment. Looting, and one or two thousand dead, that would almost be the least evil. I'm not exaggerating. This country has been completely mad for a long time. In

> any case, this time the murderers had the perfect excuse: the death of the president. I didn't dare to hope that they would be satisfied with just a little blood.[14]

However, as the genocide takes place the desire for blood continues and thousands are slaughtered not only in public places but also in sacred grounds of churches, chapels, convents, retreat centres and hospitals. The binary inversion of the power of the written and the oral communication is exchanged for the silence of those killing and those being slaughtered. In fact, killings had little of personal emotion and the killings in churches were carried out by organized groups that slaughtered many already too afraid to speak. It is here that the literary text offers an option to the colonial written world and the post-colonial oral communication by expressing divine realities and the divine presence in the silence of stillness.

According to Western understanding, it is not right to leave dead bodies unburied. In Africa, bodies decompose quickly, particularly in the humidity of Rwanda, and sickness follows. Buried bodies, on the other hand, contribute rich components to the soil; the reality is that trees and plants flourish where dead bodies have been buried. In the Christian tradition, rites of passage into the other world are celebrated before, during and after the burial of dead bodies. However, the Christian tradition also returns to the silence and emptiness of Jesus' empty tomb, an event that creates confusion among the women who were supposed to tend the tomb and the body, creating hope and resurrection out of the absence of the body and an empty silent space. The paradigm is very striking: a religious system arises out of the absence of a body that previously had been tortured and smashed onto a cross letting the body die without much companionship and in the darkness of a questioning of the purpose of all this.

It is within these reflections on buried and unburied bodies outside the well-developed doctrine of death and judgement and of the encounter between a soul and God that the insights of a theological reflection arising from the Rwandan experience become fruitful moments of theologizing. In the context of the empty tomb and the Easter encounters between the Risen Christ and his disciples, theologizing overcomes the empty tomb and the unburied body. The first task of theology is to address the very possibility of theologizing about silence and absence. Those who asked about the possibility that the resurrection was a Christian myth are vilified because for the theologians who have centred Christian faith in a resurrection and their own resurrection the emptiness and silence of Jesus' tomb does not have a purpose of a theological significance. It is after all a shell without content and the content rather than the shell provides all the answers and most of the questions. In other words, the contained has value while the container is discarded.

In the case of Rwanda, the silence arises out of the killing of the 'contained' with a demolition of the 'container' from April to July 1994; people seeking shelter inside churches are killed by destroying the walls and the doors of churches and allowing the structure to maim and paralyse while the killers double-check on any survivors after the killing. God is not to be seen while the killers destroy his dwelling places. In turn, the collapsing structures of divine existence materially destroy those who are seeking refuge in empty structures without power, without spirit, without God.

Genocide becomes no more than the systematic attempt to exclude God and his values from society so that the killers do not encounter any opposition to their plans and in their own understanding they become gods and owners of all human life around them. The numbers of those human beings killed is important, close to one million in Rwanda, six million in the Jewish Holocaust of Europe; however, the most important factor in genocide is that continuity with all institutions of the past and a cohesive society is destroyed and the protector God is excluded from any real intervention in society. God is dead because God's values given to others are crushed systematically.

In *Murambi*, the scene of God's absence is set by the return of a Rwandan, Cornelius Uvimana, who comes from Djibuti, to visit the country where his family lived before the 1994 genocide. Two childhood friends, Jessica Kamanzi and Stanley Ntaramira, meet him at the airport and they make it possible for him to visit many places including those in which people he knew and his family lived, that is, the location where they resided before they were killed. Many of their dead bodies still remain within the grounds of churches. In a visit to the grounds of the church at Ntarama Cornelius witnesses the results of the genocidal killing frenzy:

> On two long tables, inside a rectangular straw hut, human remains were exhibited: skulls on the right, and an assortment of other bones on the left. On a piece of paper caught on a little bouquet of flowers someone had written by hand, 'The innocent do not die, they rest'.[15]

After visiting a second larger building with holes left by the grenades thrown into the church by the militia, they drive to another church. At the church of Nyamata, twenty-five to thirty thousand cadavers are on display within the red brick church where Rwandan Catholics had sung and prayed to their Living God. However, in the novel the guide brings Cornelius and his friend Jessica to one of the basements of the building known as crypt number 1. Well-preserved bodies lie on tables and Cornelius is struck by one particular body that is very well preserved, a young woman, identified by the guide as Theresa Mukandori, a well-known local lady. The description of her state is horrifying but a common reflection of all the pain and suffering inflicted by torturers and killers during the genocide:

> The young woman had her head pushed back and the scream extracted from her by the pain had been frozen on her still grimacing face. Her magnificent tresses were dishevelled, and her legs wide apart. A stake – of wood or of iron, Cornelius didn't know, he was too shocked to notice – had remained lodged in her vagina.[16]

Jessica had known Theresa and had talked to her during the days before the genocide started. Theresa had said 'Jessie, they'll never be able to do anything, knowing that God can see them'. Four years later and in front of her friend's body Jessica thought 'In those days, Theresa, God was looking elsewhere . . .'[17]

Theresa's case is a typical one; her brother wanted to bury her in a decent grave but the government authorities insisted that she would make a contribution to the future of Rwanda by remaining a testimony of what had happened. Beside the church there were two graves: the first one of the priest who died before the genocide of a heart attack when he heard that Pope John Paul II was going to visit Rwanda and a second one of an Italian nun, who had given an interview to a foreign radio two years before the genocide stating that the killing of Tutsis was wrong. She was shot by unknown men and buried beside the church.[18] Later in the novel Cornelius learns that his own father, a well-known local medical doctor, was not killed but led the killings at the polytechnic in Murambi.[19] In that carnage of thousands he did not save his wife, his two children (Cornelius' brother and sister) or his in-laws. After the killings were completed he was helped to escape the scene of the crimes.

Throughout the novel it is striking that Diop and the characters he created combine a matter-of-fact approach to the killings and the events of Rwanda. More striking still is the fact that the thousands killed in churches remained unburied while others found in the countryside or the swamps were buried. The details in the novel are striking because they correspond to the reality of contemporary Rwanda in which the placement of unburied skeletons in churches and sacred places are evidence of a historical memory. God, church and nation are discussed daily because for a human being corpses, bodies and skeletons are visual images of a common humanity that suffers and of a God who remains alive or dead in the perception of human beings. Further, they remind all visitors of the social illnesses that made the Rwandan genocide possible. For most visitors, the God of Nyamata who was watching over his people remained silent while the killings were happening because he was looking elsewhere.

Indeed, while God 'was looking elsewhere' the militia not only instigated massive killings but they also took the booty of war, Tutsi women. Maybe those who were enslaved for sexual use by their captors could tell a living story if they are still alive. However, the unburied corpses described in the novel became a reality for the peace-keeping forces that tried desperately with insufficient personnel and no authority to provide safe havens for those fleeing, including the killers, or to try to diminish the military vengeance of the then army commander Paul Kagame and the victorious forces of the Rwandan Patriotic Front. However, within that carnage the bodies expressed the human understanding of an absent God while the theological reading of suffering and rape speaks still to me of a destroyed and humiliated human being who is still loved by God.

The skeletons of Rwanda tell the story of a fallen institutional Christianity and the presence of a crucified and loving God who gets killed and raped many, many times because the leaders of his own institutional church could not be there to defend him. Lt Gen. Roméo Dallaire, force commander of the UN mission to Rwanda, speaking of the forceful message provided by the dead bodies, particularly of women and girls, said:

> They died in a position of total vulnerability, flat on their backs, with their legs bent and knees wide apart. It was the expression of their dead faces that assaulted me the most, a frieze of shock, pain and humiliation.[20]

A Skeletal Theology

Why did Rwandans agree with the policy of not burying their dead? Was it because there were too many bodies? Was it because they were in shock and could not react to the possibility of grieving for all those dead? Why was the memory of the dead important to the post-genocide regime of the Rwandan Patriotic Front? These are some of the social and historical questions that arise out of a unique practice after social violence; in most other cases burial places or cremations were aimed at moving on as a nation or monuments were built in order to remember historical events. However, I am not concerned here with socio-historical explanations; I have dealt unsuccessfully elsewhere with many questions related to the 1994 Rwandan genocide. I am here concerned with theological insights, with narratives about God provided not by the Rwandan government or by those who try to understand the inexplicable but by the theologizing of a people that has to live with the bones, with the memories and with their God or the absence of God in their lives.

Most of the theologizing needs to start with the possibility of past narratives about God and bones that could enlighten the bones of Rwanda today. It is possible to articulate a theology of bones or a skeletal theology arising out of the possibility of a resurrection of the body and the understanding that was brought to Rwanda by the Catholic Church. After all, most Rwandans became Roman Catholics because of the colonial presence of the Belgians, their monarchy and their Catholicism. In the Creed recited at the Mass, believers proclaim their belief in the resurrection of the body and over the centuries the Catholic doctrine of the resurrection and personal judgement spoke of a day at the end of time when Christ would come and call all to judgement. Within that doctrinal proposition bodies needed to be preserved in one grave because the bodies were expected to be raised from their tombs in a physical manner. Cremation was not a Catholic practice until very recently because of the firm belief that bodies were going to be raised as material bodies at the end of time. Rwandans would have been taught all these truths by missionaries and would have reinforced their appreciation of material bodies that they already had in pre-colonial times.

An important text for the resurrection of the dead came late in the Old Testament and was God's promise of the resurrection of the body to the prophet Ezekiel who was asked to prophesy in the name of Yahweh as follows:

> The Lord Yahweh says this to these bones: I am now going to make breath enter you, and you will live. I shall put sinews on you, I shall make flesh grown on you, I shall cover you with skin and give you breath, and you will live; and you will know that I am Yahweh. (Ezekiel 37.5–6)

In this text the resurrection of the dead is foretold and the possibility of connecting the living and the dead made possible. It must be remembered that at the time of Jesus there was still a controversy about what actually happened to the dead and only some of the Jews believed that there was going to be a resurrection of the dead. However, the idea of a God putting flesh back on the dead was connected in Ezekiel with the Spirit of God, with the breath that was going to bring new life to that valley of the dead. The divine breath was going to do that not to heal the wounded or raise the dead as a sign to others but in order that those who were dead, without the Spirit of God, would, given a new life, believe in that God who gives life.

If the biblical vision of bones connects with contemporary theologizing, it is because there must be a divine purpose and presence among bones, a presence and action still led by the Spirit of God. I would argue that theologizing about bones is very similar to forensic work. Bones and skeletons tell a story because by examining them it is possible to know what happened. Bones show age, sickness, brokenness, strength, variety and ultimately they are a forensic extension of a human being who died. We are not used to dealing with bones any longer but those who lost loved ones in a violent manner come to terms with meeting forensic pathologists who explain at length what actually happened or could have happened to those bones when the person was alive. For example, in the context of the Chilean genocide of the opposition to General Pinochet after the 1973 military coup many were arrested, tortured and killed but many bodies were never found. Legally they were not dead but had disappeared and were called 'the disappeared'. Their relatives could not legally own their property or obtain a death certificate because they were 'un-dead'. Funerals could not be performed and rituals of burial without a body could not go ahead. Years after their abduction the families could not assert that their relatives were dead and therefore the Eucharist was celebrated to comfort the living but there could be no theologizing about the passing from this life to the next.

The touching human commonality of the disappeared of Latin America and those killed in the Rwandan genocide is that their relatives saw in the bones found after the conflict the life of their loved ones. In the case of Chile, those who were told by forensic experts that the skeleton in front of them was that of their loved one always requested a private moment with the remains in order to talk to the loved one, dead for years. Widows kissed the skull of their husbands and whole families prepared pieces of clothing and mementos of the family before the human remains were placed in a coffin and publicly buried at the national memorial to those who were killed or disappeared during the years of the military regime. The case of Eduardo Paredes gives a clear example of this practice. Paredes had been the head of the Chilean detective force under President Allende until the military coup. On the day of the coup, 11 September 1973, he was arrested at La Moneda Palace and after being a prisoner at the Tacna Regiment he was brought, together with a group of presidential aides, to Peldehue, the training ground of the Chilean special forces, where after brutal torture that included burning most of his body while he was still alive he died with all his fingers and ribs broken. His human remains were identified in 1995 and his widow and two children who lived in Sweden were told by the Chilean forensic services that his remains had been identified.

Paredes' widow and their two sons, all of Swedish nationality, arrived in Santiago and visited the Instituto Médico Legal where a forensic pathologist, Dr Hernández, explained to them what Paredes' bones had revealed. They also had the chance to see the remains, which were arranged on a metallic table in the form of a human skeleton. Eva Paredes kissed her husband's skull and spoke to him while they all cried. One of their sons, Raymundo, also spoke to the remains of his father. Dr Hernández explained that all bones were broken and burned and that the skeleton had seventeen gunshots in it.[21] Paredes' remains were sealed in a coffin into which the family put some clothes and some of their hair – symbols of their family unity and gratitude. In August 1995 over 4,000 people attended the funeral at the Santiago General Cemetery where Paredes was buried beside his daughter Camila.[22]

Rwandans shared that common love for bones and human remains because they are a bodily expression of the loved one. To a visitor all bones look the same, but relatives of those who died visit them and remain silent and in shock beside their human remains. Some relatives come often, others every day. In a quiet manner, they seem to live with the dead rather than with the living but they do not express publicly their feelings or their thoughts. Their actions provide a special meaning to the human remains.

Thus, theologizing about bones and about skeletons is to liberate the living from fear of the dead on the one hand and to show love and communion on the other hand. F. Kabasele Lumbala, reflecting on the presence of the African ancestors within the Eucharist, says:

> our African ancestors do not need the designation 'saints' to merit our veneration. They are venerable as they are, that is to say, as founders of our societies, peacemakers among human beings, inter-

mediaries between us and the Supreme Being, as forces present in our everyday life.[23]

Africans preserve a communal communication with the dead in a manner that Europeans do not – the dead are always present in the daily life of the living. In the European imagination and historical pseudo-memory the impact of the plague upon thousands who died throughout Europe made quick disposal and the burning of corpses a matter of human survival. Denying possible links between contemporary Christians in Africa and their ancestors created a complete separation between the world of the Church and the world in which Africans live daily. This lack of inculturation in African theology meant that those who killed were morally accountable neither to a silent European God nor to their ancestors. For Laurenti Magesa has recently reminded us that in Africa

> what happens to living humanity and the universe in general flows through the ancestors from God and back to God. Life – in both its positive and negative aspects – cannot therefore be conceived apart from the ancestors.[24]

Other African theologians such as Charles Nyamiti have thought of Christ as an African ancestor, founder of the African lineage of all Christians.[25]

A distinction needs to be made at this point. Bodies and human remains became unclean and to be avoided but following a pagan tradition of honouring the bodies of heroes with monuments and rites of their own in Rome and Greece Christians developed a particular hermeneutical transformation: bones of martyrs and of saints became relics and hence sacred spiritual objects rather than impure material objects.[26] Thus, during the early Christian period of widespread persecution of Christians who challenged the divinity of the Roman emperor the remains of the Christian martyrs were treasured by their companions, breaking with a Jewish tradition that stated clearly that any contact with a dead body and even the presence of a dead body made every person unclean and therefore unable to perform sacrifices and join communal prayers.[27] The idea of relics and the practice of housing them became widespread throughout the Catholic world so that 'today in a sense every Catholic church is still a reliquary'.[28] The contemporary association in Catholicism between churches, altars, relics and the Eucharist still remains part of the private sphere and the law of the Catholic Church speaks clearly about the place of relics in

Catholic life: 'The ancient tradition of placing relics of Martyrs or of other Saints within a fixed altar is to be retained, in accordance with the rites prescribed in the liturgical books'.[29]

Moreover, relics are less spoken of in an age in which the dead, bones, sacrifices and the connection with the spirits of the dead remain part of a personal understanding and are only forcefully remembered in the public sphere when soldiers die in Iraq or Afghanistan and the media are full of images of the connections between soldiers dead in combat, their loved ones and their remembrance in prayer and constructions of nationhood. Those hermeneutical public processes refer to the dead as part of nationhood while in the case of Rwanda we return to the dead as part of the communion and the life of all those who belong to the universal Christian family of the Church.

Interpreting Bones

Hermeneutics in its original form referred solely to Hermes going up the mountain and bringing to humans the messages of the gods. This original form is precisely what the hermeneutics of bones refers to: a message that comes out of the materiality of bones, bones that in the case of genocide express death and desolation, conflict and anger. Theologically, bones express a message from the gods, in the case of Rwanda a narrative of 1994. A living human being died because there was a group of killers who killed. The previous chapter dealt with the interpretation of God within the conflict. I want here to deal with the interpretation of those bones following the fruitful and very Catholic idea of relics. Relics are material objects from the past which are given a living message by Catholics for today. Yes, the hermeneutical reflections on Rwanda and the bones of Rwanda are messages of liberation for the poor and the marginalized today as the relics of martyrs were messages of hope and liberation for the earlier Christians.

Can we interpret the bones of the dead of Rwanda as relics? Or are they just the bones of loved ones, expressions of a human love of the past? In other words, is there a theological interpretation that goes beyond human love within the thousands of bones unburied within the compounds of churches in Rwanda? It is clear to me that there could be many meanings attached to the bones and that after all the process of interpretation depends on who is deriving meaning from material objects. Within the interpretation of a theology that stands back from experience, and the experience of God comes first, the interpretation of the bones follows action. The actions in this case express the care of keeping the bones, the lack of fear of those bones within the community and the love expressed by those who visit and revisit the places where the bones are kept. The hermeneutics of bones in Rwanda has become an experience of memory: ultimately, for the poor and the marginalized, for the victims of the genocide, it has become an experience of love for the memory of their relatives and for a God that has returned to Rwanda after that three months of divine absence.

I have already in the introduction to this work discussed the possible absence or presence of God. For most Rwandans, God was not present during the genocide and abandoned them. Their hermeneutics of absence was certainly highlighted by the fact that most of God's messengers, that is the foreign missionaries, left the country, protected by foreign soldiers, as soon as the killings started. It is still beyond my understanding why they left when in many other conflicts the missionaries had stayed even when they had already received death threats. However, why suggest that God was absent in Rwanda while in other cases it has not been suggested? Let it be and let the bones of the dead speak.

The poor and the marginalized are the ones who usually suffer everywhere and in every unjust situation; they remain closer to God because God is the God of the poor and the marginalized. The crucifixion of Jesus of Nazareth remains at the centre of that loving plan of embracing by the Father of all, yes, of *all*! The unburied bones of Rwanda speak of the love of God and the injustice of human society because the perception of all of them was that they would be protected inside the churches. They prayed together and they sang as the killers were coming, they comforted each other; mothers protected the young under their bodies even when the killers were smashing babies against the walls of the church. The God of the poor and the marginalized was there and remained there among those dying and those who fled from the killers. God never left them, even after the Blessed Sacrament was taken away from the tabernacle. God could not prevent the killings because God was a victim as he had been at the cross; he was in all of those who showed their love even at the moment of death. In Jon Sobrino's poignant theological analysis of victims vis-à-vis God's revelation, 'the victims of this world are the place where God is known, but sacramentally. They make God known because they make him present.'[30]

It is possible to argue that the God of Rwanda as the God of El Salvador and the God of any genocide is a silent, tranquil God who accompanies human beings in their journey. It is of his essence that he is a God that liberates but the liberation actively sought by God is a complete identification with the poor and the marginalized of society. Love for the poor and the marginalized is the first and only central act in the active silence of God within genocide because human actors have temporarily lost the possibility of creating a more human and divine society. It is the God that chooses to become fully human that is present at the moment of horrific killings within the churches of Rwanda – God is there holding a child, embracing another human being, crying for the lost humanity and the presence of evil. God has not left, has not remained untouched by the poor he showed solidarity to in the Gospels; human agency has been taken over (a common idea in an African understanding of history): a battle has taken place between life and death, themes that permeate the efforts by African theologians to understand so much death and suffering at all levels.

It is important to reiterate here that when I reflect on the love of God I am relating these very traumatic events to the action-reflection-action mode of theologizing. Thus, a God that loves all but can remain apart in moments of crisis is not the liberating God of the poor and the marginalized. A God that cannot feel the pain, the dirt and the humiliation of mothers and their children inside a church filled with corpses in Rwanda is not the God portrayed in the Gospels. That God is the God of the Old Testament but not the servant incarnation of God portrayed in the synoptic Gospels; ultimately a detached God is not the God of Christianity. That detached God is the God of Christendom and power, the God of theologies of exile where God is not in the world but accompanies at a distance, he is a God of those who still believe because they have convinced themselves that prosperity constitutes a sign of God's closeness, a theology of prosperity that is not mentioned in the Gospels or in the writings of Paul. It is the God of a misunderstanding and of a human creation, of human comfort and of human death. In Sobrino's understanding of the centrality of the cross for all Christians, 'God is present on Jesus' cross, says Paul. God is present in the poor of this world, says Matthew 25'.[31]

The experience of annihilation, prison, torture and abuse experienced by Christians in Latin America in the context of the articulation of theologies of liberation has been the parallel experience of Rwandan Christians. My experience as a Latin American who lived in a moment of genocidal repression against political opponents by the military regimes of the 1960s, 1970s and 1980s cannot allow that the God of Life is not present in moments of complete human annihilation. However, in those moments God is not watching from above, God is there as one of those who are being put through beatings and electric shocks all over the body. God is in that tortured person and the torturers desecrate a divine creation, a temple of God, at every moment in which the next wave of pain and terror arises in one's body. As I wrote in my theological reflections on the Villa Grimaldi torture camp in Santiago, Chile, that I have known well since those days of violence and chaos:

> Here, memories of the human, and bestial, scream of the prisoners also brought memories of God's voice, God's comfort and God's hope. It is clear to me that during those periods of extreme brutality, God was present, not as a witness, but as a prisoner, as a tortured and crucified body. The politics of social justice that brought many prisoners to centres of torture became the politics of God.[32]

And what about the memories of those who have to deal with the broken bones of their loved ones? What about those who had to contemplate the skeletons of those who had already departed? Departed to which place? To a better world? To heaven or hell? The victims are everywhere and those connected to the victims also become victims and loved by God. In the poignant words of Colleen Kelly, who lost a brother during the attacks on 9/11, and had to endure the probing of Dan Berrigan on her faith later:

> If we are truly interested in searching for the answer why, then the hurts of the entire world must be exposed. Like doubting Thomas's, we must probe the wounds for ourselves, slowly, deeply. We must look into the pit of Ground Zero's all over – New York, Kabul, Zion – and let our tears flow.[33]

The suffering of the victims in Rwanda or elsewhere is common, it just happens that some suffer more than others. God is with and present through all the victims. In the following chapter, I expand theological ideas on a theology of the victims, the victims of many conflicts and the ordinary victims of the everyday suffering created by consumerism and greed. It is within the realm of the victims that God lives and operates in society and it is through them that God liberates. However, within a context of Africa and of Rwanda, it is also necessary to explore the developments of African theologies with their stress on community, social and historical processes of life and death, and a very strong sense of communion with the ancestors. It is only by emphasizing the richness of Christian practice and of theological reflection in Africa that one can get away from suggesting that Africans are able to ignore God's commands completely by organizing genocide. This suggestion does not have any historical grounding if one considers the many examples of genocide and ethnic cleansing within the twentieth century, for example the Balkans, another European region, after the Rwandan genocide.[34] It is possible to suggest that high theologies that became spiritualized provide the possible grounds for a complete division between sociopolitical processes and the practice of Christianity by the faith communities. Theologies of the victims, on the other hand, could contribute to strengthen the preferential option for the poor as victims by the faith communities, an option that after all is God's option, because 'Jesus did not bear witness to just any God but to the God of the Kingdom, the God of the poor, the God of life, mercy and justice'.[35]

Notes

1 Jean Hatzfeld, 2005, *A Time for Machetes: The Rwandan Genocide – The Killers Speak*, New York: Farrar, Straus and Giroux and London: Serpent's Tail, pp. 82–3.

2 John Inge, 2003, *A Christian Theology of Place*, Aldershot and Burlington: Ashgate, pp. 1–2.

3 Felix Wilfred, 2007, 'Indian Theologies: Retrospect and Prospects, A Sociological Perspective', in Marcella Althaus-Reid, Iván Petrella and Luiz Carlos Susin (eds), *Another Possible World*, London: SCM Press, pp. 131–61, at p. 159.

4 See the sharp analysis of this historical project within the theology of Gustavo Gutiérrez in Iván Petrella, 2007, *The Future of Liberation Theology: An Argument and Manifesto*, London: SCM Press, pp. 15–16.

5 The role of the churches and of theologians at that time was to reassure Christians of their dignity and of their Christian historical project ignored and despised by the military government; see Mario I. Aguilar, 2004–9, *A Social History of the Catholic Church in Chile*, 5 vols, Lewiston, NY, Queenston, Ontario and Lampeter, Wales: Edwin Mellen Press.

6 For the history and practices of torture at the Villa Grimaldi during the years of the military government in Chile, see Mario I. Aguilar, 2000, 'El Muro de los Nombres de Villa Grimaldi (Chile): Exploraciones sobre la Memoria, el Silencio y la Voz de la Historia', *European Review of Latin American and Caribbean Studies* 69, pp. 81–8, and 2005, 'The Ethnography of the Villa Grimaldi in Pinochet's Chile: From Public Landscape to Secret Detention Centre (1973–1980)', *Iberoamericana* 18, pp. 7–23.

7 Sheila Cassidy, 1992, *Audacity to Believe*, London: Darton, Longman and Todd, p. 300.

8 Boucabar Boris Diop, 2006, *Murambi, The Book of Bones: A Novel*, Bloomington and Indianapolis: Indiana University Press, a translation of the original 2000, *Murambi, le livre des ossements*, Paris: Stock.

9 Eileen Julien, 2006, 'Foreword: An Urn for the Dead, an Hourglass for the Living', in Diop, *Murambi*, pp. ix–xii, at p. x.

10 Mario I. Aguilar, 2008, *The History and Politics of Latin American Theology*, vol. 3, London: SCM Press, pp. 180–83.

11 Éloi Messi Metogo, 2006, 'Bible and Liturgy', in Éloi Messi Metogo (ed.), *African Christianities* (*Concilium* 2006/4), London: SCM Press, pp. 56–61, at p. 58.

12 Jung Mo Sung, 2007, *Desire, Market and Religion*, London: SCM Press, p. 3.

13 For a critical literary analysis of *Murambi* see Fiona McLaughlin, 2002, 'Writing the Rwandan Genocide: Boucabar Boris Diop's *Murambi, le livre des ossements*', in Toyin Falola and Barbara Harlow (eds), *Palavers of African Literature: Essays in Honor of Bernth Lindfors*, vol. 1, Trenton, NJ and Asmara, Eritrea: Africa World Press, pp. 203–20.

14 Diop, *Murambi*, p. 11.

15 Diop, *Murambi*, p. 71.

16 Diop, *Murambi*, p. 73.

17 Diop, *Murambi*, p. 73.

18 Diop, *Murambi*, p. 74.

19 Diop, *Murambi*, pp. 76–7.

20 Lt Gen. Roméo Dallaire, 2004, *Shake Hands with the Devil: The Failure of Humanity in Rwanda*, London: Arrow Books, p. 430.

21 See 'Resumen del estudio médico-legal de los restos de Eduardo Paredes Barrientos, República de Chile, Ministerio de Justicia, Servicio Médico Legal, Unidad de Identificación, Características de la osamenta Protocolo No. 2885/91, 10 Julio 1995' (Oscar Soto, 1999, *El ultimo día de Salvador Allende*, Santiago: Aguilar Chilena de Ediciones, pp. 241–2).

22 Percival Cowley V. ss.cc., 'Homilía en los funerales de Eduardo Paredes Barrientos' (Soto, *El ultimo día de Salvador Allende*, pp. 243–8).

23 F. Kabasele Lumbala, 1998, *Celebrating Jesus Christ in Africa: Liturgy and Inculturation*, Maryknoll, NY: Orbis, p. 47.

24 Laurenti Magesa, 2004, *Anatomy of Inculturation: Transforming the Church in Africa*, Maryknoll, NY: Orbis, p. 112.

25 Charles Nyamiti, 1988, 'The Naming Ceremony in the Trinity: An African Onomastic Approach to the Trinity', *African Christian Studies* 1988/1, pp. 41–73.

26 For a general description of these changes in perceptions of human remains and bones see James Bentley, 1985, *Restless Bones: The Story of Relics*, London: Constable.

27 David Sox, 1985, *Relics and Shrines*, London: George Allen & Unwin, p. 16.

28 Bentley, *Restless Bones*, p. 213.

29 *Codex Iuris Canonici* 1983 Can. 1237 § 2.

30 Jon Sobrino, 1994, *Jesus the Liberator: A Historical-Theological Reading of Jesus of Nazareth*, Tunbridge Wells: Burns & Oates, p. 251.

31 Sobrino, *Jesus the Liberator*, p. 251.

32 Mario I. Aguilar, 2008, *Contemplating God, Changing the World*, London: SPCK, p. xi.

33 Colleen Kelly, 2002, Foreword to Daniel Berrigan, *Lamentations: From New York to Kabul and Beyond*, Lanham and Chicago: Sheed & Ward, pp. xi–xiv, at p. xii.

34 For a history of several European processes of ethnic cleansing see Manus I. Midlarsky, 2005, *The Killing Trap: Genocide in the Twentieth Century*, Cambridge: Cambridge University Press.

35 Sobrino, *Jesus the Liberator*, p. 268.

3

Public Theology from the Periphery

The failure of the churches and the theologians to condemn the ethnic discrimination that led to the genocide in Rwanda brings to all of us the urgent task to construct a theology of liberation that allows the victims and the theologians to speak. This chapter explores contemporary understandings of public theology in relation to other types of non-European theologies that could be labelled public; for example, the theologies that come under the umbrella of Latin American theologies or liberation theologies. The first part of this chapter explores the possibilities of public theologies within the centre/periphery axis, while the second part argues for a relocation of public theologies towards the periphery; specifically, Latin America and Africa. In the aforementioned continents, the public face of Christianity in numbers and influence is growing, while Christianity in Europe continues to decline. In its final part, the chapter examines the theology of 'the crucified' and 'the victims', within the Latin American context of the writings of Jon Sobrino, by pointing to theological continuities and discontinuities in Latin American theologies vis-à-vis European public theologies.

From South Africa to the World

At the start of the twenty-first century it is clear that public theology has become the face of the theological world. Indeed, it has become the face of theology due to the decrease in numbers of congregations and institutional Christianity within Europe. Thus, a deeper engagement by theologians with the world of politics has taken place because the European churches need to find a voice within ever more secularized and diversified policies. Some would say that this situation is forced upon the churches and that the churches are fighting for survival as public bodies within contemporary society.

I would argue the opposite: the churches have always engaged with relevant social and political issues; however, the face of theology as understood by the public has been the study and development of systematic theology; an argumentative interpretation of the doctrines of God and the Church as a body that engages with the world from a doctrinal point of view. This is not the reality any longer. On the one hand, the churches in Europe have become bodies engaged fully in political discussions about particular public policies but without the influence on the public that they had in the past; on the other hand the churches in North America and Latin America have become ever more central to the conversations between the state and the public and, therefore, public theology has become a centre-stage partner of democratic conversations.[1]

The growth of Christianity in Latin America, Asia and particularly Africa has brought a globalized public face to Christianity, in which the periphery of the European churches has become the centre of growth, the centre of worship and the centre of a public theology.[2] This chapter deals with those changes by arguing that the centre/periphery axis of common goodness has shifted and that the process of theologizing has diversified. Within those changes, I would argue, public theology becomes crucial, not as a normative way of doing theology, but as a contextual way of theologizing within the growing centres of Christianity, where the victims of social injustice, globalization and natural disasters do not have the same rights and the same social services enjoyed by citizens of the European Union and industrialized countries.[3]

It is on this theological axis that the possibility of rethinking African theology after Rwanda, and indeed all theologies as public theologies, becomes central for liberation. The example of South Africa, and particularly of Archbishop Desmond Tutu, showed that South African churches and their leaders were instrumental not only in ending the structural sin that was apartheid but also in the development of a national reconciliation that led to the building of a new South Africa. Thus, theology and liberation for the twenty-first century provide continuity between a Latin American liberation theology, an African theology of liberation and the Christian response to conflict and interreligious strife within Asian theologies. For the continuity of a theological project as part of a 'historical project' in Africa requires the hope that Christians in Africa, as was the case of a few within Rwanda, continue proclaiming the Good News of God's liberation. However, the Good News is to be announced within the liturgical celebrations of African inculturation as well as within the public arena of involvement in contemporary political activity on behalf of the poor and the marginalized that constitute the majority of the African population. For the cry of Jean-Marc Éla is still valid after the experience of Rwanda; he wrote:

> While people wallow in misery, we are centring our reflection and action on religious rites and customs! As the gospel comes face-to-face with African traditions, we must find another way to understand and live our faith. Perhaps we ought to ask ourselves whether the attraction of the sects does not reside precisely in the disappointments suffered by men and women who refuse to identify with Christianity as it is lived in our churches.[4]

The example of Desmond Tutu as a public figure that prayed and led worship but never ignored the plight of the poor and the oppressed is a good example of the kind of response to national crisis that was expected in Rwanda. Despite the fact that it would have led to a civil conflict of major proportions, it would have alerted the international community and the African Union to the impending national collapse that was to take place in Rwanda.[5] For Rwanda's genocide took place at the same time that South Africa was becoming a new nation under the leadership of the former political prisoner Nelson Mandela and with the backing of Tutu's moral authority.

The role of the churches within South Africa became very prominent with Tutu as General Secretary of the South African Council of Churches (SACC, 1978–85).[6] The SACC had 20 member churches and four observer member churches and represented 15 million Christians with the exclusion of the churches that advocated a white-only membership.[7] By 1979 the SACC passed a resolution that advocated civil disobedience in response to apartheid laws.[8] Tutu had been deeply touched by a little girl that explained to him that she lived with her widowed mother and sister; according to the little girl, they had no income whatsoever and when hungry, they borrowed food, when no food was available they filled their stomachs with water.[9] In December 1979, Tutu assessed the situation for the benefit of the Anglican Provincial Synod of South Africa, taking as his starting point a reflection on Jesus and his ministry and the prayerful life of Anglican communities and reaching the following conclusion:

> It is precisely our encounter with Jesus in worship and the sacraments, in Bible reading and meditation, that force us to be concerned about the hungry, about the poor, about the homeless, about the banned and the detained, about the voiceless whose voice we seek to be. How can you say you love God whom you have not seen and

hate the brother whom you have? He who loved God must love his brother also.[10]

On 24 February 1988, the South African Government outlawed seventeen anti-apartheid organizations and violence escalated. Already the previous year, Tutu in a visit to Maputo had stressed the possibility of martyrdom and the fact that, at one point or another, the use of violence against an unjust regime was justified. On 29 February, church leaders met at Cape Town and marched arms together in a single file towards the Parliament building, an action that was illegal under South African law. They numbered 150 and as they faced a police contingent they knelt and sang hymns.[11] The police arrested the leaders and used water cannons to disperse the rest, ending the day with mass arrests. The foreign media quickly reported that a new era had begun as church leaders took to the streets to protest against the regime. They later called for a protest rally on 13 March 1988 that was banned by the government.

In 1989, President P.W. Botha resigned and there were hopes that a negotiated settlement could be reached, particularly because the public protests were increasing as ambassadors from 12 European nations had met with church leaders and were putting ever more pressure on the South African government to comply with international standards of equality, law and finances. In February 1990, the new President, F.W. de Klerk, proclaimed the end of apartheid, authorized the existence of the ANC and the PAC and released Nelson Mandela, political prisoner number 1. Despite the increasing degree of violence, South Africa held its first democratic and non-racial elections in April 1994, electing Nelson Mandela as President of South Africa in a coalition that included the NP and the Zulu Inkatha Freedom Party (IFP). During that month, as South Africa proclaimed a new liberation for all, the Rwandan genocide started. Hence, the need to address the centrality of theology as public *res* and as a narrative about God that needs to be heard in the public places.

Relocating Public Theologies

In their seminal collection on public theology, William Storrar and Andrew Morton argue that 'public theology has to do with the public relevance of a theology which has at the core of its Christian identity a concern for the coming of God's Kingdom in the public world of human history'.[12] Together with that statement, they embrace two particular positions when it comes to the role of public theology; those of Jürgen Moltmann and Duncan Forrester. For Moltmann, 'a *theologia publica* . . . becomes political in the name of the poor and the marginalized in a given society'; for Forrester, public theology 'offers convictions, challenges and insights derived from the tradition of which it is a steward, rather than seeking to articulate a consensus or reiterate what everyone is saying anyway'.[13]

These particular statements make a close link between public theology, or rather public theologies, and those theologies that arose out of the peripheries of the European-centred theological world in the 1960s.[14] Indeed those public theologies and their practitioners managed to bridge the change imposed by the changing world of modernity, in which doctrinal statements became isolated and ignored. The role of the emerging churches after the crisis of Vietnam and the challenges of nuclear deterrents became central within the world.[15] Those challenges were not part of confrontational statements, but were included within participatory alignments through social and political discussions that encouraged fresh dialogue not only between churches and the state, but also within different Christian traditions, as well as between world religions and those with no faith at all.[16] I would even argue that, if public theology had been more prominent, there would have been a smaller decline in numbers and less increase in secularism within European nations that 30 years ago were not under the political control of the former Soviet Union. Public theologies provide processes of dialogical theologizing that in turn question structures of ecclesial authority, by assuming that church and world are closer than in any systematic theological thinking. For Marcella Althaus-Reid, they provide new agendas for doing theology and for being church, so that:

> In theological terms, it means a serious disruption and redistribution of power, and of strategic institutional thinking. The task of public theology is precisely strategic, by providing a space for the people who are integrities in dissent at the margins to engage in a network of thinking and sharing experiences.[17]

Moreover, the move of public theology from the centre to the periphery is not inconsistent with Moltmann's or Forrester's statements; it calls for a rethinking of the public/private, centre/periphery, inclusive/exclusive and religious/political categories of our theologizing, as well as the centre/periphery axis for theologizing in a globalized community.[18] Peripheries are dangerous: margins are not centres in which to remain, because the danger is that God could be moving as well.[19]

Relocation of centres and peripheries are not like urban/suburban developments in which landscapes are resettled; relocation of centres and peripheries moves theologizing from centres to peripheries and vice versa. Thus, the experience of theologizing at a desk is different from the theologizing of those working in parishes. It follows that the theologizing within European centres of learning and European centres of theological action and public theology is different from the process of theologizing at the centre of the victims, the periphery of the European Union or the margins of the world.[20] A further complexity arises due to the fact that peripheries of injustice and oppression do exist within the industrialized nations as well as within the 'Third World' nation states.

To summarize this first section, the localized sense of a public theology as the engagement proposed by Moltmann and Forrester provides a certain rich commonality to a theological world connected by churches, institutions and theological faculties, in which theologians share a Christological confession and a sense of the Church as an instrument of Christ in the public world of social ethics, politics and the state. However, it is appropriate at this juncture to ask: Is this a context in which public theology can remain during the twenty-first century and within an already globalized Christianity and an ongoing process of globalization? My answer to the question is 'no', and I would like to explore the possibilities of a globalized public theology, without universally accepted norms and with contextualization without exclusion, through the relocation of public theologies, considered thereafter as diverse ways of theologizing, always remaining within an axis of faith communities-state-public.

Relocating Public Theologies

Two processes seem to permeate the complexity of public theology: reinvention and relocation. By reinventing public theologies new subjects and themes arise, as society and the world change. By a natural process of relocation, public theology tends to regroup within ecclesial structures and to reassess possible subjects of theologizing. Both processes are plausible and theologically agreeable. However, my own preference is for a process of relocation, of change and exchange of the role of the theologian and the possibilities of creating narratives about God (theology) within a globalized community and particularly within the centres of Christianity located in Latin America, Africa and Asia.

Elsewhere, I have developed a detailed process of ordering elements for theologizing at the periphery; suffice it to say here that I have argued that the theological peripheries of the past are the theological centres of today and that theologizing at the periphery requires a commitment on the part of the theologian to share the values of the Kingdom of God with the poor and the marginalized.[21] The change has come not only because of the decline in Christian practice in Europe but, most importantly, because of the developments within a political and, therefore, a public theology in the Third World. John de Gruchy has reminded us that 'there is no universal "public theology", but only theologies that seek to engage the political realm within particular realities'.[22] Further, the phrase 'political theology', as used by Johann Baptist Metz and Jürgen Moltmann, refers to a European theology and certainly not a theology of the periphery; it nevertheless challenges the disengagement of theological thinking with the world and Metz particularly emphasizes the authority of God vis-à-vis the suffering of the world in the context of east–west relations and a north–south divide.[23]

Within the Latin American theological context, the process of theologizing has been marked by a situation very different to that encountered by other political theologies, but that nevertheless fulfilled the characteristics given at the start of this chapter for public theologies. Even so, by the 1970s the Latin American engagement between the political and the religious – between the churches and the state – had become determined by a declining democratic way of life, in which the values of a democratic unity and community are undermined by the creation of national security states – supported by the United States – and with emerging military leaderships that, at the same time, proclaimed themselves Christian.[24] In a sense, the Latin American nation state was a victim of the Cold War; ordinary citizens were part of somebody else's concerns and somebody else's wars. Regardless of their position vis-à-vis the state (support in Argentina and opposition in Chile), the churches had to develop a public profile in which all doctrinal statements had to be conceived in terms of a violent situation and the possible restoration of democratic systems.[25]

Through that process theologizing became a political act and a public manifestation of belief during times of persecution and violence. Theologians had less time to write their theological works in offices, while the immediacy of the gross human rights violations polarized the churches and the states. In 1968, the Latin American bishops meeting at Medellín, Colombia, questioned the validity of unjust societies in Latin America and requested a full reinvention of the nation state in line with gospel values, since the majority of Latin Americans professed the Christian faith.[26] The act of writing theology became secondary to the act of theologizing; the poor and the marginalized became the centre of theological activity, with action (praxis) coming first and theology (reflection) coming second.[27] The hermeneutical circle was extended to include the context of the poor and the oppressed and a new kind of public theology from the poor and the marginalized started to arise. Jon Sobrino calls them 'the crucified people' and 'the victims'; the subjects of God's love and the prime producers of narratives about God in Latin America.[28] It is on the axis of victims–church–state that we must look for a public theology in Latin America, because after all a *theologia publica* not only speaks for the poor, as suggested by Moltmann, but arises out of the life of the poor and the marginalized.[29]

Two Types of Public Theology

The idea of a public theology from the victims is an attractive heuristic device, in order to forward a possible understanding between European theology and all those Latin American theologies that I have classified under the larger single umbrella of liberation theology and/or liberation theologies.[30] Liberation as a heuristic device provides a metaphor for a theology that challenges unjust structures within Latin American society, in the same way that public theology challenges Europe. However, Latin American theology, as 'a second act', comes out of the experiences of the God of Life within the experience of marginalization.[31] As Pablo Richard argues:

> the world of the poor contains a mystery: here, God personally comes to meet us and to bestow a self-revelation. The world of the poor is now seen for what it is: the privileged locus of the presence and revelation of God.[32]

Here I want to return to an argument developed by the Uruguayan theologian Juan Luis Segundo, who in a talk in Toronto in 1983 surprised his audience by suggesting that there are two kinds of liberation theology; that is, there are two ways of doing theology in Latin America.[33] In Segundo's assessment of liberation theology, Gutiérrez and others developed a theology of liberation ten years before Gutiérrez's seminal work *A Theology of Liberation* (1971) was published, which coincides with the Second Vatican Council.[34] In one of its most important statements, Vatican II located the concerns of the Church within the world and embraced the realities of all, rather than treating Church and world as separate social realities. Thus, the *Pastoral Constitution on the Church in the Modern World* asserts that:

> The joy and hope, the grief and anguish of the men of our time, especially of those who are poor or afflicted in any way, are the joy and hope, the grief and anguish of the followers of Christ as well. Nothing that is genuinely human fails to find an echo in their hearts.[35]

The influence of Vatican II within Latin America, where the majority of Christians consider themselves Roman Catholics, was enormous.[36] However, the initial thrust of a written liberation theology was to influence the young middle classes, who were attending universities; later, it developed new insights into the usual systematic theological themes and much later communicated those developments to the theologically uneducated masses. In the difficult context of military regimes and the Medellín conference, a new group of theologians decided to move towards the periphery; they started learning from the poor and the marginalized and, as a result, started a second and somehow different project of liberation. For Segundo, both groups made an enormous contribution to the development of Latin American theology, but they created a contradiction within the hermeneutics of the cross, because the poor, for the most part, accept suffering as part of God's plan and deal with it through so-called 'popular religiosity' in their everyday life.[37] The middle classes, however, challenge injustice and appropriate the voice of the poor in their sociopolitical movements by excluding the poor.

One could say that Segundo's comments arose out of his pastoral experience and daily contact with educated lay people, rather than popular sectors of society, as with Gutiérrez's experience in the slums of Lima.[38] Thus Segundo was able to problematize the methodology used by liberation theologians and alert others to the contradiction inherent in speaking of a monolithic liberation theology in which theology is related to orthopraxis rather than orthodoxy.[39] Segundo concluded that the theologian of liberation does not advocate anything other than orthodoxy, but that orthodoxy and the hermeneutical suspicion exercised by a theologian always requires the use of the sciences of the past – history – as well as those of the present – sociology – in order to develop thought and ongoing critiques vis-à-vis theological methodologies for Latin America.

If one takes Segundo's comments seriously – few commentators have – the theological thinking that comes out of the educated groups within Latin America relates directly to a European public theology, in that the role of theology and the role of the public theologian is not only to deal with matters concerning church and state, but the public – the masses of people, who in European society represent tax payers and in Latin America represent the educated middle classes, professionals, office workers and those who in general have a say in the running of the state. It is through Segundo's distinction that one can sense the social injustice towards the majority of the Latin American population that, even within the public realm, is excluded from participating in the church–state–public axis. As a result, a central difference between public theology and a Latin American theology, in Gutiérrez's sense, arises: European public theology aims at engagement with the educated public and starts with the professional theologian, whereas a Latin American public theology arises out of the communitarian reflections of the ecclesial communities – parishes organized in basic Christian communities – and ultimately discusses the bare minimum aspirations of the poor – the majority of the population rather than the possibility of an ethical sharpening of an already well-running democratic system that grants equal rights and obligations to all its citizens.

As a result of their different contexts, the role of the public theologian in Europe and Latin America is rather different. The role of a theologian, and particularly a public theologian, becomes dependent on the issues that are taking place on the church–state–public axis, regardless of the possibilities of speaking in public about theologizing. Thus, the location of the theologian matters for the process of theologizing and here a further distinction between European public theology and the Latin American one arises. Within Latin America the theologian is within the communities of Christians that in general are involved within Sobrino's first type of theologizing, that of Gutiérrez and the periphery of the slum. However, if one were to locate Segundo's groups of professionals or university students within the world of public theology, or a scholarly theology that deals with the world of the public, Latin American theology would still be considered by European public theologians to be at the periphery of the globalized centres of learning located in Europe or in North America.[40]

The act of theologizing at the periphery suggests, by its mere location, that it is a political act that challenges the injustice and centrality of the state and develops, through a committed action with others, a symbolic meaning, a political meaning and a Kingdom meaning. In doing so, the political activist comes closer to God, because s/he openly proclaims the centrality of God as just, as active, and as present on the periphery, ultimately challenging the centre. Public theologians take part in that process of community theologizing, centred on the values of the Kingdom of God, that challenge contemporary ill-distribution of wealth or lack of social services within twenty-first-century nation states in Latin America. Thus, theologizing becomes a utopian activity, because in reality there is little hope that social structures or political processes are going to change throughout Latin America, particularly with the globalized financial policies implemented by the World Bank and the International Monetary Fund.[41] The public theologian adheres to the utopian values of the Kingdom of God, while living the Christian utopia at different levels within society vis-à-vis the crucified people and the victims of a process of globalization, global warming, economic injustice and war.

A Utopian Public Theology of the Victims

The process of theologizing starts at the periphery and returns to the peripheral location of the Kingdom of God as anti-poem, anti-market and anti-value. Theologizing becomes political activism, because it has started from a social action in solidarity that has led to a further emptying of the self. The altruistic process of peripheral solidarity then can have four circular and related processes, bearing the characteristics of both community and individual.

First, altruistic solidarity with the self; that is, because of circumstances an individual or a community becomes involved in a process of cooperation; solidarity with others within a very localized periphery. Second, altruistic solidarity with a group, such that the actions and reflections of that particular group within the periphery build up a Christian anger at an unjust situation and a common theologizing takes place; avenues of hope and utopian understandings of the Kingdom of God take place. As a result the group decides to have a *caminata*; to journey towards the centre of power in order to challenge the status quo. Third, altruistic solidarity with those unknown, whereby the actions and reflections from the periphery and already expressed at the centre create an altruism of solidarity with others who are marginalized and others whose problems are not of concern to any group or individuals in the localized periphery category. Risks and political activities related to the Christian values of the Kingdom of God are taken, in order to help others rather than ourselves; these actions differentiate altruistic attitudes and actions from organizational and structural empowering. Fourth, altruistic solidarity from the centre towards the periphery; that is, the periphery remains the centre of political activism and religious solidarity; however, members of the centre join the periphery not because they suffer the same problems but because they yearn for an altruistic life based on the values of the Kingdom of God.[42]

The process of theologizing, the geographical location of the theologian and the utopian cycle of altruism in service and solidarity can then be compared with the ideal of service of the leaders of a church and of the politicians in government. Those ideals are sometimes not realized, because of the implementation of policies that run contrary to the Christian values of the Kingdom of God. Those values put utopia and service at the forefront of human society, making, in the context of Latin America, a particular choice for the majority of the public; that is, for the poor and the marginalized – victims of social injustice and natural disasters – within society.

It is here that the theology of the victims maintained by Sobrino explains the connection between the 'private' world of the anonymous victim and the public statement of a theology that not only argues for the support the victims need, but places the victims and the crucified at the centre of the process of theologizing. First, the crucified peoples of Latin America had to endure decades of injustice by military governments aligned to the powerful warlords of a new empire, and the voices of the victims became embodied in the statements by public theologians – most of the liberation theologians – and by the public theology of Archbishop Oscar Romero of El Salvador. Romero, by experiencing the suffering of the poor, became their voice and, even when assassinated in March 1980, rose as a public figure who symbolized the ultimate sacrifice of a committed Christian and an honest public theologian. Second, the advent of democracies brought freedom of speech to those who had been silenced by the military regimes; however, they became victims of economic policies associated with the new phenomenon of globalization.

Globalization, described as a network of international communication that provides better cooperation between peoples of the world, is nevertheless regulated by laws on trade and exchange and rules of cooperation.[43] All those rules are set up from above, by certain powerful nations, in order to regulate their economic growth and their view of the world, rather than the needs or aspirations of the two-thirds of the global population that still live in poverty. Free trade agreements, for example, are seen as a triumph by nations in the south of the planet, because Latin American nations are able to bring their goods to North America and Europe. However, a small nation like El Salvador receives in return US goods from private companies that sooner or later dominate the economy and dictate the policies of further trade and economic growth. Within the international involvement in the US 'war on terror', for example, El Salvador was the only Latin American country to send troops to Iraq, because they could not reject the US administration's petition to join the US-led coalition, since most of their national income comes from the United States, particularly from money sent by Salvadorians living in the United States to relatives in El Salvador – financial transactions that the US could block or tax heavily.[44]

For Sobrino, the voice of those who support and protect the victims of globalization is central to them, because the powerful and rich of this world are not going to defend their interests. The values of the Kingdom of God do not conform to the values of globalization, where the opening of markets and the creation of wealth (capital) are of the essence for the rich nations. Instead, the values of the Kingdom as portrayed in the Gospels show Jesus of Nazareth welcoming all, particularly the poor and the marginalized, comforting the victims and providing ever more food when needed, not for a few friends but for all those listening to him. The centrality of globalization provides a market in which all eyes are centred on those who can produce the best businesses and the best transactions, those considered economic celebrities and revered as role models for others. Indeed, they could be role models for those in the rich countries, but not for the majority of humanity. Within this kind of public theology of the victims, the values of the Kingdom of God challenge role models and, within the high theology of the Gospel of John, the crucified draws all things to him (Jn 12.32; 19.37).[45]

In Sobrino's reflection the crucified and the victims are the ones who bring salvation, because they are part of a globalized truth of a common humanity drawn by God; rather than part of a humanity that seems to be part of those who have, while 'two billion human beings live on less than two dollars a day, half of these on less than one'.[46] The excluded of this world are the signs of what Ignacio Ellacuría calls 'the civilization of poverty'; a globalized humanity living in common poverty (that is, lacking the basic necessities of life) but living in peace and harmony with each other. Thus, for Sobrino, 'placing the suffering of victims at the centre of the "globe" leads to truth and the universalization of human values. This has nothing to do with "victim culture" but with the need-invitation to respond to the victims with *mercy and justice*.'[47]

The future of the process of globalization, according to Max Stackhouse, 'could promote a highly pluralistic global civilization with increased prospect for peace with justice'; however, he also remarks that 'it is unlikely to happen unless it finds its focus in Christ as Lord, for

Christ is the one who has, and can, renew the covenant between God and humanity, and point souls and societies towards Jerusalem'.[48] The global realities of 9/11, the war on terror and the Iraq war have probably watered down the globalized utopian sense of a common purpose, expected by Stackhouse in the first part of his statement. Nevertheless, the second part of his statement has become extremely important. The fact is that the tension of globalization–victims–covenant has drawn together public theologians and their theology with an ongoing process of assessing the relation between countries where Christian theology is well established and their impact on other countries affected by larger processes of globalization. It would suffice to say that a globalized coalition fighting in Iraq has been more successful in bringing nations together than those trying to unify a Christian response to those globalized alliances. It is a fact that the US administration manipulated the notion of a Christian civilization versus the Islamic world, with a clear choice for Christian fundamentalism, avoiding the possibility that globalized coalitions could help the victims and the crucified of the world, not only those located in Latin America but elsewhere too.[49]

The notion of Christ as Lord, and as the one who can renew the covenant between God and humanity, presupposes a common humanity ready to accept that notion. It is clear that a common humanity is not ready to accept that option, even when a theological division is made between the Jesus of the Gospels and the cosmic Christ that embraces the rest of humanity, in their public and ritual response to the love of God. Thus, it is surprising to find that Third World theologians, in the final common statement of their meeting in Mexico in 1986, argue that:

> Jesus reveals God, but does not limit or exhaust the divine. In the light of the risen Jesus and the cosmic Christ, nothing prevents God's self-revelation to all God's people. It is liberating to confess that God is not confined to Christian traditions, churches, and scriptures. Wherever God makes self-disclosure and self-gift, the word enters the earth, becomes embodied in history, participates in people's struggles for justice and freedom, and helps propel them toward their (up)rising and liberation.[50]

Within that theological option, God is at the centre, revealing his love and presence to humanity and, particularly, to those within the world religions living out of the socio-historical context of Asia. It is the covenant between God and the created world that stands at the centre; a covenant between God and humanity, God and nature and the different realms of the cosmos where the human victims live. Thus, the wise words of the fourteenth Dalai Lama – a respected religious voice for the victims and a victim himself – resound strongly as he speaks of human beings and a common humanity, rather than of markets and flows of information. In the words of his Nobel Prize Lecture in 1989:

> I am always reminded that we are all basically alike: we are all human beings. Maybe we have different clothes, our skin is of a different colour, or we speak different languages. This is on the surface. But basically, we are the same human beings. That is what binds us to each other.[51]

Dialogue with world religions is crucial here, because the victims of globalization are part of larger symbolic globalized communities; namely, the world religions. It is a common front of globalized public theological statements on peace that could bring a larger and richer engagement between the churches, the state and the general public. In many ways Christian leaders and Christian public theology are doing that; nevertheless, unless we become self-centred the relation between victims and inclusion in a public theology engaged with theologians from all the world religions becomes crucial for the development, not of a unified, universal or normative public theology, but a globalized and victim-centred public theology. In the words of Leonardo Boff: 'It is within this context that we, Christians, must remember our origins as excluded and crucified. As an act of solidarity, we must always recount this historical event.'[52]

There is no doubt that public theology has become central to processes of theologizing and solidarity with the poor and the marginalized in the twenty-first century. Processes of globalization and the ever increasing numbers of Christians in Latin America and Africa have somehow relocated the possibilities of an effective globalized and diversified public theology. Thus, it is possible to argue that public theology, in a diverse contextual arena outside Europe, will become increasingly central to the development of theology in the future. The contextual differences will provide a diversified public theology in a globalized Christianity; however, those diversified public theologies will also maintain a certain continuity, shaped by the churches–state–public axis, in contemporary processes of globalization based on the typology of altruistic solidarity developed in this chapter; ultimately, solidarity and a public theology based on the altruistic values of the Kingdom of God, a concept/reality central to Latin American theologies and

African theologies since the genocide in Rwanda, which is the subject of the following chapter.

Notes

1 The fastest growth of Christianity is taking place in Africa; however, the political influence of the churches in Africa is less significant than that of the churches in Latin America. This may be linked to the weaker ecclesiology found in African Pentecostalism compared to Roman Catholicism. See Ludovic Lado SJ, 2006, 'African Catholicism in the Face of Pentecostalism', in Éloi Messi Metogo (ed.), *African Christianities* (*Concilium* 2006/4), London: SCM Press, pp. 22–30.

2 After the end of the military regimes that coincided with Vatican II, the Latin American churches which had been active in moving towards democratization (not in Argentina) continued to have an important role within national reconciliation and the development of truth commission; see Iain S. Maclean (ed.), 2006, *Reconciliation, Nations and Churches in Latin America*, Aldershot and Burlington: Ashgate.

3 Democratization has become part of the open and growing field for public theology: 'there is today, then, a convergence between the democratic *system* and its *vision*, and the ecumenical *koinonia*, its holistic missionary paradigm, and its vision of *shalom*'; John W. de Gruchy, 1995, *Christianity and Democracy: A Theology for a Just World Order*, Cambridge: Cambridge University Press, p. 276 (original italics).

4 Jean-Marc Éla, 1994, 'Christianity and Liberation in Africa', in Rosino Gibellini (ed.), *Paths of African Theology*, London: SCM Press, pp. 136–53, at p. 137.

5 For a fuller assessment of contemplation and politics in the life of Archbishop Tutu see Mario I. Aguilar, 2008, *Contemplation and Political Activity*, London: SPCK, chapter 5.

6 For a history of the SACC and the development of the different Christian traditions in South Africa see Marjorie Hope and James Young, 1981, *The South African Churches in a Revolutionary Situation*, Maryknoll, NY: Orbis.

7 The World Alliance of Reformed Churches General Council meeting in Ottawa on 25 August 1982 endorsed many other previous declarations by national Reformed bodies and reiterated 'its firm conviction that apartheid ("separate development") is sinful and incompatible with the Gospel'. See 'Racism and South Africa: Statement adopted by the General Council in Ottawa on 25 August 1982', II.1; full statement in John de Gruchy and Charles Villa-Vicencio (eds), 1983, *Apartheid is a Heresy*, Cape Town and Johannesburg: David Philip and Guildford: Lutterworth Press, pp. 168–73.

8 On complex ruptures within Christianity in South Africa see John W. de Gruchy, 1997, 'Grappling with a Colonial Heritage: The English-speaking Churches under Imperialism and Apartheid', in Richard Elphick and Rodney

Davenport (eds), *Christianity in South Africa: A Political, Social and Cultural History*, Oxford: James Currey, Berkeley: University of California Press and Cape Town: David Philip, pp. 155–72.

9 John Allen (ed.), 1994, *Archbishop Desmond Tutu: The Rainbow People of God*, London and New York: Doubleday, p. 26.

10 'We drink water to fill our stomachs: Address to the Provincial Synod of the Church of the province of Southern Africa 1979', text available in Allen (ed.), *Archbishop Desmond Tutu*, pp. 27–41, at p. 31.

11 For an excellent overview of churches involved in sociopolitical issues during this period see Tristan Anne Borer, 1998, *Challenging the State: Churches as Political Actors in South Africa 1980–1994*, Notre Dame, Indiana: University of Notre Dame Press.

12 William F. Storrar and Andrew R. Morton, 2004, 'Introduction', in William F. Storrar and Andrew R. Morton (eds), *Public Theology for the 21st Century: Essays in Honour of Duncan F. Forrester*, London and New York: T&T Clark, pp. 1–21, at p. 1.

13 Jürgen Moltmann, 1999, *God for a Secular Society*, London: SCM Press, p. 1 and Duncan B. Forrester, 2000, *Truthful Action*, Edinburgh: T&T Clark, pp. 127–8.

14 I discuss theological typologies of the single and the plural in Mario I. Aguilar, 2007, *The History and Politics of Latin American Theology*, vol. 1, London: SCM Press.

15 Nuclear deterrents became part of a public theology that was assumed to be central to the discourse on common humanity; thus, US and UK churches were not ignored despite nation states' decision to build nuclear weapons; see John XXIII, 1963, *Pacem in Terris* and National Conference of Catholic Bishops, 1993, *The Harvest of Justice is Sown in Peace*, Washington: USSC Office for Publication and Promotion Services.

16 Important practitioners of an inter-faith public theology were the American monk Thomas Merton and the exiled Tibetan leader the fourteenth Dalai Lama. See Joseph Quinn Raab, 2006, 'Comrades for Peace: Thomas Merton, The Dalai Lama and the Preferential Option for Nonviolence', in Victor A. Kramer and David Belcastro (eds), *The Merton Annual: Studies in Culture, Spirituality and Social Concerns* 19, Louisville, KY: Fons Vitae, pp. 255–66.

17 Marcella Althaus-Reid, 2004, 'In the Centre There are No Fragments: *Teologías Desencajadas* (Reflections on Unfitting Theologies)', in Storrar and Morton (eds), *Public Theology for the 21st Century*, pp. 365–83, at pp. 381–2.

18 See Mario I. Aguilar, 2008, *The History and Politics of Latin American Theology*, vol. 3, *A Theology of the Periphery*, London: SCM Press.

19 See Marcella Althaus-Reid, 2001, 'The Divine Exodus of God: Involuntarily Marginalized, Taking an Option for the Margins, or Truly Marginal?', in Werner Jeanrond and Christoph Theobald (eds), *God: Experience and Mystery* (*Concilium* 2001/1), London: SCM Press, pp. 27–33.

20 See 'How Ought We To Preach the Cross in a Crucified Society Today?', in Leonardo Boff, 1988, *When Theology Listens to the Poor*, San Francisco: Harper & Row.

21 Aguilar, *The History and Politics of Latin American Theology*, vol. 3.

22 John W. de Gruchy, 2004, 'From Political to Public Theologies: The Role

of Theology in Public Life in South Africa', in Storrar and Morton (eds), *Public Theology for the 21st Century*, pp. 45–62, at p. 45.

23 See Johann Baptist Metz, 1997, *Zum Begriff der neuen Politischen Theologie 1967–1997*, Mainz: Matthias-Grünewald, and Jürgen Moltmann, 1984, *Politische Theologie: Politische Ethik*, Munich: Kaiser, cf. Jürgen Moltmann, 2000, *Experiences in Theology: Ways and Forms of Christian Theology*, London: SCM Press.

24 See Jeffrey Klaiber SJ, 1998, *The Church, Dictatorships, and Democracy in Latin America*, Maryknoll, NY: Orbis.

25 See Mario I. Aguilar, 2004–6, *A Social History of the Catholic Church in Chile*, vols. 1–3, Lewiston, NY, Queenston Ontario, and Lampeter, Wales: Edwin Mellen Press.

26 See Second General Conference of Latin American Bishops, 1970, *The Church in the Present-Day Transformation of Latin America in the Light of the Council II Conclusions*, Washington, DC: United States Catholic Conference (USCC).

27 '[P]ractice refers to action in a particular sector of human life, such as educational practice, while praxis is made up of the entirety of human practices in the social realm'; João B. Libânio, 2000, 'Praxis/Orthopraxis', in Virginia Fabella, M. M. Sugirtharajah and R. S. Sugirtharajah (eds), *Dictionary of Third World Theologies*, Maryknoll, NY: Orbis, p. 172; see also Gregory Baum, 1999, 'The Impact of Marxist Ideas on Christian Theology', in Gregory Baum (ed.), *The Twentieth Century: A Theological Overview*, Maryknoll, NY: Orbis, London: Geoffrey Chapman and Ottawa: Novalis, pp. 182–3.

28 Jon Sobrino, 1993, *Jesus the Liberator: A Historical-Theological Reading of Jesus of Nazareth*, Tunbridge Wells: Burns & Oates, pp. 254–71.

29 Clodovis Boff, 1993, 'Epistemology and Method of the Theology of Liberation', in Ignacio Ellacuría SJ and Jon Sobrino SJ (eds), *Mysterium Liberationis: Fundamental Concepts of Liberation Theology*, Maryknoll, NY: Orbis and North Blackburn, Victoria: Collins Dove, pp. 57–85.

30 Mario I. Aguilar, 2007, *The History and Politics of Latin American Theology*, vol. 2, *Theology and Civil Society*, London: SCM Press.

31 See Gustavo Gutiérrez, 1984, 'The Task of Theology and Ecclesial Experience', in Leonardo Boff and Virgil Elizondo (eds), *La Iglesia Popular: Between Fear and Hope* (*Concilium* 1984/6), Edinburgh: T&T Clark, pp. 61–4 and Raymond Plant, 2001, *Politics, Theology and History*, Cambridge: Cambridge University Press.

32 Pablo Richard, 1993, 'Theology in the Theology of Liberation', in Ellacuría and Sobrino (eds), *Mysterium Liberationis: Fundamental Concepts of Liberation Theology*, pp. 150–68, at pp. 150–51.

33 Juan Luis Segundo SJ, 'Two Theologies of Liberation', Toronto, 22 March 1983, in Alfred T. Hennelly (ed.), 1990, *Liberation Theology: A Documentary History*, Maryknoll, NY: Orbis, pp. 353–66.

34 See Robert J. Schreiter, 1999, 'The Impact of Vatican II', in Baum (ed.), *The Twentieth Century: A Theological Overview*, pp. 158–72.

35 Second Vatican Ecumenical Council, 'Pastoral Constitution on the Church in the Modern World *Gaudium et Spes*' (7 December 1965), § 1.

36 The sessions of the Council (1962–65) were followed by the strong state-

ment of economic policies, articulated by Paul VI in *Populorum Progressio* (1967), summarizing dependency theories and incorporating ideas relating to dependency theologies; Josep Ignasi Saranyana (ed.), 2002, *Teología en América Latina*, vol. 3, *El siglo de las teologías latinoamericanistas 1899–2001*, Madrid: Iberoamericana and Frankfurt am Main: Vervuert, pp. 258–60.

37 The phenomenon of 'popular religiosity' is a socio-religious continuum within Latin America. See Fourth General Conference of the Latin American Bishops, 1992, 'New Evangelization, Human Promotion and Christian Culture: *Santo Domingo*', § 38.

38 See 'Gustavo Gutiérrez', in Mario I. Aguilar, 2007, *The History and Politics of Latin American Theology*, vol. 1, chapter 1.

39 Juan Luis Segundo SJ, 1976, 'Theology and Popular Religions', in *Liberation of Theology*, Maryknoll, NY: Orbis, pp. 183–207.

40 See Pablo Richard with Margaret Hebblethwaite, '*The Tablet* Interview: Speaking for the Church in a New Language', *The Tablet*, 9 June 2007, pp. 6–7.

41 Leonardo Boff, 2005, *Global Civilization: Challenges to Society and Christianity*, London: Equinox, pp. 21–4.

42 This theological typology is taken from Aguilar, 2008, *The History and Politics of Latin American Theology*, vol. 2, chapter 8.

43 C. T. Kurien emphasizes that 'the defining aspect of globalization . . . is the relationship, at all levels, between human beings and capital, their own creation', see 'Globalization: An Economist's Perspective', in Storrar and Morton (eds), *Public Theology for the 21st Century*, pp. 195–212, at p. 210.

44 Elson Concepción Pérez, 'El Salvador, Irak . . . y las remesas de la guerra', *Las Dos Habanas/Cuba*, 20 July 2004, Elson Concepción Pérez, 'El Salvador podría enviar más tropas a Irak', *La Prensa Gráfica/Prensa Latina*, 1 December 2006 and Elson Concepción Pérez, 'Prevé El Salvador permanencia de tropas en Irak en 2007', *Diario de Chiapas*, 28 December 2006.

45 Jon Sobrino, 2001, 'Redeeming Globalization Through its Victims', in Jon Sobrino and Felix Wilfred (eds), *Globalization and Its Victims* (*Concilium* 2001/5), London: SCM Press, pp. 105–14, at p. 108.

46 Sobrino, 'Redeeming Globalization', p. 109.

47 Sobrino, 'Redeeming Globalization' (original italics).

48 Max L. Stackhouse, 2004, 'Public Theology and Political Economy in a Globalized Era', in Storrar and Morton (eds), *Public Theology for the 21st Century*, pp. 179–94, at pp. 190–91; see also Max L. Stackhouse et al. (eds), 2000–7, *God and Globalizatio*, vols 1–4, Harrisburg: Trinity Press International/Continuum.

49 See 'The Political Fundamentalism of Bush and of Bin Laden', in Leonardo Boff, 2006, *Fundamentalism, Terrorism and the Future of Humanity*, London: SPCK, pp. 35–6.

50 See the document based on the Seventh International Conference of the Ecumenical Association of Third World Theologians, 'Commonalities, Divergences, and Cross-Fertilization Among Third World Theologies' (7–14 December 1986), § 65, in K. C. Abraham (ed.), 1990, *Third World Theologies: Commonalities and Differences*, Maryknoll, NY: Orbis, pp. 207–8.

51 The fourteenth Dalai Lama, 1990, 'The Nobel Peace Prize Lecture, Oslo,

Norway', in Sidney Piburn (ed.), *The Dalai Lama: A Policy of Kindness – An Anthology of Writings by and about the Dalai Lama*, Ithaca: Snow Lion Publications, pp. 15–25, at p. 15. The connections between Thomas Merton and the Dalai Lama are important, because Ernesto Cardenal and the new foundation of the Trappist monastery in Santiago were all connected through discourse influenced by Merton; see Mario I. Aguilar, 2008, *Contemplation and Political Activity*, London: SPCK, chapters 1 and 2.

52 Boff, *Global Civilization*, p. 63.

4

Post-Colonial African Theology and Liberation

This chapter examines some contemporary trends and methodological developments in African Christian theology, particularly processes of ordering and subsequently disordering as a particularly African theological method. Its framework suggests that colonialists and theologians shared a common purpose, i.e. ordering. As a result, theology and colonialism developed related methodologies of ordering knowledge. It is these processes of ordering/disordering that could help us understand and theologize about the 1994 Rwandan genocide and the place of God in all those moments and particularly in a post-colonial theology. For it is in a post-colonial era that a process of theological disordering is taking place led among others by Kabasele Lumbala's conception of the body within liturgical theology in an African context.

The initial development of African theology as a particular body of research and writing coincided with the processes of independence from colonialism by many African nations in the mid-twentieth century.[1] Further writings were triggered by the missionary churches' reflection on gospel and culture, the influence of the Second Vatican Council on the African Catholic Church and the challenges to Christianity by the growing number of independent churches in the continent.

Within Christianity in Africa three types of theology became recognizable: mission theology, African theology and black theology (South African theology). Within those theologies, two themes became central: the relation between theology and politics and that between theology and African culture.[2] However, the diversity of African theologies provided a common purpose in searching for an African Christianity that could be expressed through an African liturgy and communal life. Such African Christianity would be the result of an ongoing theological reflection on the biblical text, the African cultural context and the many African expressions of Christian Churches and Christianity in general. As a result, diverse African theologies responded to different moments of social life and developed into a theological rainbow, where the totality provided a clearly visible phenomenon of theological action and reflection, using multiple methodologies. As a result, it is no longer possible to talk about an African theology but only of African theologies, that is, theological works that have arisen out of the reflection on African realities by well-educated clergy or committed Christians with high levels of literacy and intellectualism.

This chapter examines some contemporary trends and methodological developments in African Christian theology, particularly processes of ordering and subsequently disordering as a particularly African theological method, so as to understand the historical background to which Kabasele Lumbala is providing a response. Following John Mbiti's distinctions, I explore the subject of written African theologies, rather than 'oral theology' or 'symbolic theology'.[3] I suggest that colonialists and theologians shared a common purpose of ordering. As a result, theology and colonialism developed related methods of ordering knowledge. In the case of colonialism, a complex science of ordering territories and peoples was developed. Such ordering included Western education as a system of ordering minds, bodies and souls according to the models used in Europe.

In challenging a theological system with a European cultural background, African theologians used an initial process of disordering. Thus, the search for new theological concepts within Africa can be considered and will be explored in this chapter as a process of disordering. Through such a process European-based philosophical and theological ideas were contested and later rephrased and reordered. Theologians such as Charles Nyamiti have suggested a model of adaptation of European theologies and a theology from above based on the possibility of contextualizing theological formulae and the development of theology in Europe within Africa. Kabasele Lumbala on the contrary has suggested that it is through the communal celebration of the liturgy that theologies from below and local narratives of faith are constructed. Thus, theological truths and contextual assumptions encounter each other in a disorderly manner.

It is clear that within that cycle of contemporary order and disorder, African cultural ideas of society and self have been central as methodological tools for the processing of ordering theology in an African context. Thus, African ideas related to history and the Christian history of salvation, community and communion, ancestors and kin, sacraments and sacramentals, signs and symbols have challenged the idea of a God that was not present or was not working in Africa before the arrival of colonial officers and missionaries.

In the first part of this chapter, I explore colonial representations of peoples in need of conversion, the idea of the peoples without history and the process of colonizing the mind. In the second part, I explore some foundational assumptions proposed by African theologians immediately after the colonial period. In the third part, I explore the use of a non-linear history by African theologians in order to develop a theological paradigm that runs parallel to the history of Christianity in Europe. In the final part, I examine the Christocentric paradigm of the world of the living and the dead, emphasized by Nyamiti and Kabasele, in order to suggest that contemporary African theologies have provided a local theological order, basically Christocentric, and centred in community rituals. It is within those communal rituals that the theological work of Kabasele makes sense.

Eventually, such order will have, once again, to be challenged and made disorderly. However, such African *gnosis* (*gignoskein* = to know) currently connects European Christian practices with African ones, through a process of ongoing relatedness. *Gnosis* explained as 'seeking to know, inquiry, methods of knowing, investigation' and even 'acquaintance with someone' differs from *doxa* or opinion, and from *episteme* as 'both science and general intellectual configuration'.[4]

This chapter's conclusions suggest that the use of African historiography, African social history, and African philosophy has provided a central epistemological paradigm for a future development of African theologies. As the lives of peoples in Africa continue changing, such a historical paradigm will create a firm grounding for theological models that will develop further understandings of the presence of God through the Christian communities in Africa.

The Ordering of Minds

Valentin Mudimbe has suggested that colonialism was a science of ordering implemented by explorers, colonial administrators and missionaries. European explorers aimed at filling the gaps on maps of Africa, and indeed of the world. In the name of monarchical states, explorers searched for rivers and forests with incomplete maps that centred the world in Europe, where civilization and culture existed. Once explorers had reported on what they had found – lakes, rivers, mountains and peoples – colonial administrators were sent to take possession of lands that remained, according to Europeans, without owners, uncivilized and untamed.

As a result, the colonial machinery became fascinated by the diversity of peoples and by the fact that nothing much was known about them. Since the promulgation of the bull *Inter caetera* (1493) by Pope Alexander VI, the mandate to overthrow paganism and to establish the Christian faith in pagan nations had been implemented by Christian European kings. *Dum diversas* (1452) and *Romanus Pontifex* (1455) had granted the king of Portugal the right to embrace Muslims, pagans, enemies of Christ and Africans in general as his subjects and possession. The Reformers' challenge to the Pope's instructions was quickly followed by the application of European principles of religious practice: *cuius regio, eius religio.*

Africa like other territories was considered *terra nullius* (nobody's land), and the scramble for Africa in 1895 followed former practices. Those departing for Africa occupied territories by taking them as possession of kings, by ordering them and by bringing Christian faith and European knowledge to those who did not have it. The Christian revival of the nineteenth century followed the end of the age of Enlightenment with its criticism of religion, and following the first Vatican Council theological doctrines within Catholicism were reordered. Missionaries followed the theological paradigms of the nineteenth century by sending personnel in order to save souls and to build up the Kingdom of God. The 'cursed continent' of Africa was also called to be an orderly part of a Church associated with monarchies and with God's plan of salvation. *Interior Africa solemnis gaudii proximi Ecclesiae triumphi particeps fiat* – 'the interior of Africa may participate in the solemn coming joy of the Church's triumph'.[5] The Church was planted, was built and in some cases flourished among peoples that in many cases associated missionaries with colonial functionaries. Towns were built with colonial administrative centres and Churches or Christian missions.

However, within such missionary expansion (justified by the mandate given by monarchs and in the case of the Catholic monarchies by the Pope himself) missionary education became central to the colonial paradigm of ordering. Religious instruction was central in the mission schools; however, the way to be Christian taught at the mission schools was European, and therefore to become an educated Christian was to acquire European dress and a European way of behaviour.

Those educated in mission schools were taught European history and the Christian history of salvation. As a result 'dark Africa' remained a continent without a past, while the peoples of Africa remained 'peoples without history'. Such assumption of the absence of any African history was supported by European philosophers such as Hegel, who overemphasized the centrality and primacy of the European self in his *Lectures on the Philosophy of History*.

For Hegel, world history is the self-realization of God (a theodicy), reason and freedom, a process leading to enlightenment, i.e. 'the development of the consciousness that the Spirit has of its freedom and also the evolution of the understanding that the Spirit obtains through such consciousness'.[6] Thus, for Hegel, development (*Entwicklung*) determines the movement of a concept (*Begriff*) into an idea.[7] However, universal history moves from east to west, so that 'Europe is the absolute end of Universal History'.[8]

The influence of Hegel and Kant cannot be overlooked. Thus, Hegel's assessment of Africa's development in history and the realities of the Spirit among Africans can come as a shock to contemporary readers. Hegel writes: 'Africa is in general a closed land, and this maintains its fundamental character'.[9] And further, 'The realm of the Absolute Spirit is so impoverished among them and the natural Spirit so intense that any representation which they are inculcated with suffices to impel them to respect nothing, to destroy everything . . . Africa does not have history as such. Consequently we abandon Africa, to never mention it again. It is not part of the historical world; it does not evidence historical movement or development.'[10]

As a result of such writings, oral African histories and any African past were overruled by European social mores and their primacy while Christian attitudes conflicted enormously with local African customs and beliefs about the world and the action of God in the world. The colonization of African minds was at the centre of the educational system and with few exceptions newly converted African Christians were expected to think differently from other Africans and to behave in different cultural ways.

When Europeans attributed this lack of history to Africa, they tried to erase the long-established process of African *gnosis*, in order to replace cosmological systems of social and religious knowledge with a European *episteme*. Christianity in its European cultural form produced a religious discourse that followed an epistemological fallacy. Such a fallacy (that the continent of Africa had not encountered or responded to Christianity in the past) could not be supported historically. The history of Africa included the presence of Tertullian, Cyprian and Augustine in North Africa and the rapid development and establishment of Christianity in Ethiopia.[11]

Thus, history as 'an intellectual effort of ordering human activities and social events chronologically' is also 'a discourse of knowledge and a discourse of power'.[12] In the words of Michel Foucault, history has the 'project of bringing man's consciousness back to its real condition, of restoring it to the contents and forms that brought it into being, and elude us within it'.[13] Michel de Certeau observes that 'in history, which leads from the subject of mysticism in the sixteenth century to the subject of economics, primitive man lies between the two. As a cultural (or even epistemological) figure, he prepares the second by inverting the first, and, by the end of the seventeenth century, he is erased, replaced by the native, the colonised, or by the mentally deficient.'[14]

Therefore, the first task of a post-colonial independent Africa was a much-needed reconstruction of an African history. The independent movements that became part of the newly formed independent African nations of the twentieth century stressed the value of African societies, their cosmologies, their customs, their systems of knowledge, their emphasis on community and their central religious values, practices and attitudes. The principle of disordering applied to the colonial order was also applied to a European missionary theology. Moreover, for African theologians it is clear that the challenge to European systems of order suggested that the methodologies of ordering used within colonialism had failed to understand the foundations of African societies. Ngindu Mushete, for example, has concluded that

> One clear fact has obviously escaped western humanity for a long time. It is that there is not *one* world but *many*, not *one* history but *many*, not *one* theology but *many*, not *one* space or milieu but *many* that are different and perhaps even antagonistic.[15]

The Disordering of Theology

In this section, I explore the critique of missionary theology, theologies of adaptation and European theology. Within this period are established the foundations of what African theology could be in relation to European missionary and colonial theology. This period coincides with the end of colonial rule, the rise of economic elites and neo-colonialism in Africa. Central to its understanding are the challenges posed to colonial missionary activity by, among others, the Second Vatican Council and the European restructuring of thought and social action by the protests in Paris during 1968.

During the colonial period, the emphasis on missionary theology had created a confrontation between European Christianity and African life and rites. Two seminal works provided the first critiques of such a state of affairs. A Belgian missionary, Placide Tempels, published in 1945 *Bantu Philosophy*, in which he explored the possibilities of an African view and explanation of the world and of the action of God in such a world that would differ from the European one.[16] Following such work a group of African priests, who can be considered the pioneers in African theology, produced a collection of essays, *Des Prêtres noirs s'interrogent*, through the publication *Présence Africaine* in Paris (1956). They asked questions about inculturation and liberation within Christianity and Africa and challenged the accepted missionary theology of that time, without agreeing completely with a theology of adaptation.

It was the theology of adaptation that became prominent within the first period of African theology, a period from the end of the colonial era to the creation of the Ecumenical Association of African Theologians in 1977 (in Accra). A theology of adaptation encouraged the adaptation of the practice of Christianity in Africa. It was still a Eurocentric perspective, but it moved a step forward from the *terra nullius* ideology applied to Christian churches and their African communities previously. The final statement of African theologians in Accra suggested a resourceful theological reflection that was not trying to adapt European Christian practices to Africa, but came out of a historical reflection on the social and political realities of Africa from the perspective of a Christian commitment. African theologians wrote,

> For this we need an interdisciplinary methodology of social analysis, biblical reflection, and active commitment to be with the peoples in their endeavors to build a better society.[17]

It is clear that at this juncture of its development, a very strong critique of European thought and systematic theology is present in the writings of African theologians who belonged to an already post-colonial and neo-colonial world. For example, Kofi Appiah-Kubi suggested that

> Our question must not be what Karl Barth, Karl Rahner, or any other Karl has to say, but rather what God would have us do in our living concrete condition. For too long African Christian theologians and scholars have been preoccupied with what missionary A or theologian B or scholar C has told us about God and the Lord Jesus Christ.[18]

However, within that post-colonial period, African theologies recognized that contradictions were present within the post-colonial world of varied *epistemes* and disorderly *gnosis*. Sergio Torres, for example, reminded African theologians that

> We belong to the educated class of our countries and easily adopt its style. We live physically in the Third World, but our houses, our books, our way of life, are British, French, American. How many of us actually live with the poor and share their experience? How many of us work with the workers and peasants as companions in the struggle?[19]

Within this period the foundations for a critical African theology were provided. Those methodological assumptions included the following *epistemes*:

1 Theology has a living historical character, so that all theology is culturally and socially positioned. As a result, 'the notion of a universal theology, like that of a universal philosophy, is a myth'.[20]
2 African theological language has its source and foundation in the Bible.[21] It follows the theological realization of other theologians working in the Third World that 'a theology that does not act on behalf of the poor and the oppressed is not Christian theology'.[22] Within this episteme of an African Christian theology, there is no exclusion towards other forms of African theology, such as discourses about God arising out of indigenous religious forms, Islam, or urbanized forms of non-conformist Christianity, such as the widespread phenomenon of the African Independent Churches.
3 History becomes a tool for theology, history understood in its sacred and secular spheres.[23] In that way, 'the God of history speaks to all peoples in particular ways'.[24] Such contemporary view of history proposes a history that moves in two spheres of discourse, 'the traditional Western canon of history as *res gestae*' (what happened) and the historiography 'beneath mere events'. Within this second historical paradigm Africa and its peoples are reconstituted as the starting point of history, rather than (as formerly) the starting point of missionary and colonial history.[25]
4 African theology has a cultural context, the diverse cosmological world-views of African peoples, societies and nations. In those diverse views, 'the whole creation is defined as a life-death conflict'.[26]
5 African cultures are to be recognized as the particular locations of God's presence. Within those *loci* Africans do not operate a Greek concept of being, as individual, but have a dynamic perception of community, people in relation, not only with the living, but also with the dead, the spiritual beings and the founding ancestors of clans, lineages and ethnic groups.

6 African perception, conceptions and constructions of space and time are to be recognized as central for the understanding of life and death and the world where God intervenes. Time is cyclical and not linear, thus 'existence and time move in repeated and endless cycles'.[27] The spirit world is a mirror of the world of the living and what differentiates the dead from the living is their form of action in society. Thus, the living prepare to join the dead, who do not live in separation from the living. Space is multi-dimensional, with God and the supreme beings in the sky, patron gods and nature spirits live on earth and ancestral spirits live in the world beneath. Evil spirits move around the world because they did not achieve a peaceful transition from the world of the living to the world of the dead.
7 Liturgy or worship is a community activity, where members of such community communicate and keep in touch with the multidimensional spaces through a sacred passage of time. Thus, 'worship is an elaborate series of manipulative rituals designed to harness the resources of good deities in order to ward off the machinations of the evil spirits and to control space-time events'.[28]
8 Humanity as present in Africa is defined in the context of community. Just as it has been in traditional religion, humanity is to be conceived as 'being in relation'.[29] Therefore, individual knowledge and awareness come from the community. For Africans, life is a life-in-community, and therefore, according to Mercy Oduyoye, 'our nature as beings-in-relation is a two-way relation: with God and with our fellow human beings'.[30]

The search for different ways of asking questions from the social and religious realities of Africa provided comprehensive summaries of the theological task ahead. Interestingly enough, those agendas were communally addressed by theological faculties, pastoral institutes and the publication of theological journals.

African Christian theology was written by priests and ministers of religion, while lay people took part more actively in related areas such as experimentation with liturgical rites and the discussion of missionary theology and that of the Small Christian Communities. Some women theologians such as Mercy Oduyoye brought new perspectives on women and their realities in Africa, providing theological discourses on fertility, motherhood and a feminist critique to a male dominated Christian tradition in Africa. The process of disordering provided a firm challenge to the former colonialist theology and at the same time gave impetus to further questioning on the possible and still absent relation between African theology and contemporary European bodies of theological writings in the late twentieth century.

An African Paradigm of Historical Theology

When the first written works of African theology started to be published in the twentieth century, there were questions posed about the relation between Christianity and the indigenous religions of Africa. If Christianity embodied a particular body of revelation, how was it possible to develop any Christian theology in Africa outside this body of writings? Those who proposed the Christian history of salvation as the only base for African theology, *qua* Christian theology, made a distinction between African Christian theology and the theology of African Traditional Religion (ATR).

Muzarewa, for example, makes that clear distinction, suggesting that 'African theology is done by Christians for the Church and is based on the Bible, it is Christian theology and differs substantively from *traditional* theology in Africa'.[31] Fashole-Luke follows the same argument, but suggests that there is no African theology outside the biblical text.[32] However, Mbiti suggests that African Christian theology is interchangable with African theology.[33] For Agbeti, there is a clear distinction between African Christian theology and African traditional theology: Christian theology is Christocentric while traditional African theology is theocentric.[34] The relation between both kinds of theology seems to be clearer, as African traditional theology can be perceived as a '*preparatio evangelica*'.[35]

Within all those distinctions that are certainly not a matter of semantics, it is important to recognize that indigenous African traditions and Christian practices are both present within Africa today. Thus, the term African Traditional Religion seems to suggest a static system of beliefs and practices. That is not the case. African indigenous traditions change and respond to concrete contemporary problems of life and death. The same can be said of an inculturated and historical African Christian theology.

Christ and the Ancestors

Once the issues of an African history as part of salvation history had been cleared, African theologians could proceed to move forward in a more systematic way. Such systematization explored mainly the role of Christ as centre of revelation within an African context, while still recognizing the diversity of African theologies. Robert Schreiter has suggested that such explorations of the person of Christ for African Christianity not only help build an ever-growing body of African theology, but also make 'distinct contributions to the understanding of Christ for the whole Church'.[36]

Within such richness of Christological inculturation, I will examine two African theologians and their theological approximations to the person and role of Christ in Africa. It can be argued that the Christological paradigms of Charles Nyamiti and François Kabasele Lumbala have become prominent in contemporary African theology and have provided two important paradigms in liturgical theology and systematic theology.

Nyamiti has linked a more systematic and dogmatic Christology within the African discourse on Christ and has opened avenues for variety in African Christology. Kabasele Lumbala has wrought his theology from the richness of culture and has asked questions about an African Christology that comes from the Christian experience of community in a particular African locality and that is expressed through liturgical rites as Christological events.

Nyamiti's theology has managed to call to order other theological efforts.[37] In fact, though several authors have contributed to the largest area of theological research within Africa, Nymiti's efforts have challenged their lack of a *nexus mysterium*. Thus, if all Christian mysteries are indeed interconnected, Christological research could provide further understanding of one particular mystery in the light of others. For Nyamiti, the central question 'Who is Christ for the African?' cannot be properly answered without knowing who Christ is in himself.

Such a theological paradigm of interconnection has provided a bridge of dialogue between European Christologies and African ones. As a result, theological assessments of Nyamiti's work have already been published in Europe.[38] Those who criticize Nyamiti's work have suggested that he has used traditional theological concepts in order to develop something that comes out of African experience and therefore needs some fresh epistemological concepts in order to expand. The strength of Nyamiti's model arises out of his sense of a theological tradition and the construction of African theology and Christology as a continuation of a universal theological tradition.

Kabasele Lumbala's Ancestral Christ

François Kabasele Lumbala, a Catholic priest from the Democratic Republic of Congo (formerly Zaire), studied in Paris and completed doctorates in liturgy from the Institut Catholique and in religious studies from the Sorbonne. He teaches at the Catholic Faculty of the University of Kinshasa, and at the theological seminary of the Oblates of Mary Immaculate.

Kabasele's model of an African Christ intends to bridge the European division between the human and the sacred, and suggests the vindication of the human as the place where God acts in the world and where the African Christ is likely to be more meaningful. As in the case of Nyamiti, Kabasele's work centres on his own tradition, and he examines the African perception of the human in the sacred by way of the celebration of the sacraments.

As noted by commentators outside Africa, most of the African theologians within the Roman Catholic tradition use theological ideas outside their tradition, and have developed an ecumenical theology. Therefore, if Kabasele explores the relation between liturgy and inculturation within the Congolese Church and communities, he is effectively suggesting that within this context the sacraments are celebrated and are requested by the majority of the Congolese population.

Kabasele differs from the more universalistic theology of Nyamiti in that he is aiming at a close examination of seven sacraments, i.e. baptism, confirmation, Eucharist, marriage, reconciliation, anointing of the sick and ordination, within a particular tradition.[39] His ordering and disordering aims to provide symbols within the Catholic liturgy that can express the presence of Christ for Africans, as understood by Africans themselves.

François Kabasele Lumbala has maintained that it is in the African liturgy and through the worship of local African communities that indigenous African cultural elements can and must be incorporated. The centrality of such liturgical practice assumes that the theology of inculturation reflects a way of doing theology that comes out of experience, an African experience of the spiritual and material worlds. Such experience is manifested and expressed through the body and it is subsequently lived and written by faith communities that reflect kinship and symbolic networks within a particular social history.

Together with other African theologians, the Congolese Kabasele Lumbala shares the experience of having being ordained as a Catholic priest in 1974, when the new liturgical rites in the Catholic Church had already been revised. After ordination he worked at a parish in

Cibombo, Zaire; he continued his pastoral ministry in Paris for five more years later on. His doctorates in theology (liturgy, Institut Catholique Paris) and in comparative religion (Sorbonne) provided a sound grounding for his theological investigations after his studies, but also reflected his own concerns as an African Christian and as a Catholic priest.

Most of his writings have been produced in the French language. The journal *Concilium* has been instrumental in making his ideas known in the English-speaking world.[40] The liturgy is central for him, as it is for Vincent Mulago with his works on symbols and sacraments.[41] His theoretical use of the body as the place where God and people meet, and where cultural gestures and divine communication express an African Christian experience and reflection, is unique among African theologians.

However, other African theologians have challenged the centrality of the liturgy suggested by Kabasele Lumbala. For example, Jean-Marc Éla (Cameroon) has noted critically that 'while people wallow in misery, we are centring our reflection on religious rites and customs!'[42] Éla has further suggested that a traditional Africa with its rich cultures cannot be used as a contemporary parameter of theological reflection, because it remains in the colonial past. Instead, the situation of oppression and poverty within Africa suggests that liberation is what is needed. This critique of Kabasele Lumbala's cultural and liturgical presuppositions reflects another manifestation of a theology of inculturation in Africa, where the post-colonial experience is perceived as a universal challenge to oppression and a theological response of liberation from sin. Our sinful condition is understood as part of the individual or community, as well as part of society's structural and economic sin.

The experience of the South African theologians during apartheid is important here. They certainly challenged the narrative that created an unequal society with the Black majority not being able to access resources.[43] However, this reflection was filtered by Christian communities who celebrated their Christian life in the shanty towns and produced South African theologies closer to the North American Black theologies that had confronted inequality in civil rights based on colonial narratives of slavery and Christian white supremacy.[44]

Moreover, in analysing Kabasele Lumbala's contribution to theology, I assume that the variety of those African theologies and the constant challenge among them comes from the fact that social and religious contexts do change. Those different social and cultural situations can produce different theological emphases because the incarnation of Christ creates a salvific paradigm centred in different histories and moments of that universal history. Thus, addressing Éla's concerns, one could say that it is through processes of liberation and their liturgical celebration that God becomes part of an African cultural experience. The concern for inculturation in the liturgy does not exclude, instead it includes, processes of Christian liberation through cultural freedom and the use of contextualized theological paradigms.

Further, the mystery of the incarnation as portrayed by Kabasele Lumbala requires a certain interest in the milieu that Jesus chose for his life. It was there that the incarnate Word of God transcended Jewish culture, so that according to Kabasele Lumbala 'in the Incarnation, God has seen to it that the pathways of humanity converge, but God has done so only by going beyond them, always transcending all models'.[45] As we cannot understand the incarnation solely in one cultural setting, there is no doubt that the fact that Africans or any other people can celebrate their faith using gestures, symbols and actions that they understand has already brought a new freedom to liturgical development.

This process of inculturation relies on a theological reflection that tries to rediscover the presence of God in the history and customs of Africa. Cultural traits and the creation of an ethnotheology remain central to any process of inculturation. The assertion that 'yesterday's Africa is no more' contradicts the daily experience of most Africans. They have to deal with sickness and death in terms of indigenous conceptions that depart from Western conceptions of the body, this world and the other, or life and death in general. Regarding the social body, Kabasele Lumbala asserts that human beings are located beings and that Christianity as a way of life cannot exist outside a cultural location.

While politics and economics are certainly part of contemporary Christian concerns by Africans, Kabasele Lumbala stresses the priority of a liturgical theology over a liberation theology. This priority is based on the African experience of the past – when the management of the temporal becomes the main concern of the Church, 'we may doubt the Christian authenticity of the Church'.[46] Doubt arises when church leaders and Christian leaders are seen as too involved in temporal matters. After all, governments can change and economic policies can vary, but cultural traits within an expanding Christian celebration of life provide continuities, community and a unity between the material and the spiritual.

Kabasele Lumbala has strongly suggested that lay Christians should be encouraged to participate in the political world. However, the grounds for such social and economic liberation from poverty and oppression start with the liberation from the cultural oppression that was the norm during the colonial period in Africa. Therefore, 'the African rituals . . . have introduced into Christian worship a perception of life and the world different from the bottom line of classical Christian theology. This conception is one of a world constructed as a place of participation in life coming from God as the ultimate reality and summit.'[47]

An Inculturated Theology of the Body

The inculturation of African liturgies has incorporated dance, movement, oral narratives instead of readings, blessings, acclamations, drums etc. It has been a process that from the outset has provided exciting liturgies with lots of participation, particularly at the offertory and at the moment of community acclamations. Nevertheless, African liturgies have also reflected cultural understandings and the voice of Africans themselves who have chosen for example to call Christ a Chief, an Ancestor and an elder brother.[48]

At a theological level, Kabasele Lumbala has suggested that till very recently the body has been repressed. After all, the body constitutes an expression of God, it acts as a mediator of God's life and it constitutes a visible sign of those who are members of a particular community. In Western philosophy the body and the soul are divided, and therefore in Western theology they remain divided in their liturgical expressions. In such liturgical theology, the body relates to other members of the community during the liturgy, but most of the time the body expresses the individual movement of a single soul towards God and vice versa.[49]

Instead, within African societies and for contemporary African Christians the body or parts of the body represent a human being. For example, 'to save a human being is to save body and soul together. A human being is entirely in a fingernail, a hair, a flake of skin.'[50] In other words, 'a human being is a "signifying body" situated in time and space'.[51] This body is used to divide the natural and the supernatural and to mark ritual moments that are sacred because they allow the divine and the human presence to converge in a particular place, in a particular moment, in a particular community.

In those ritual and sacred moments Africans exchange their daily activities for ritual moments; however, they do not become passive recipients of blessings or graces. Instead, they become participants in community. The only way they can become participants is by using their bodies, by effecting gestures, by exchanging gifts, by dancing, by clapping, by adorning themselves with colours and substances, by allowing God to speak through signs, symbols, actions and bodies in community.[52]

The analysis of different ways of celebrating rites of passage, ritual moments, religious professions, blessings and sacramentals allows Kabasele Lumbala to suggest that 'Christian liturgy is not a finished book whose pages one turns to find the only valid tones and words. It is history on the move, a history of love that must ceaselessly find the apt gesture, the right word, the pregnant symbol that fit the situation.'[53]

Such analysis challenges past liturgical uniformity and missionary education. The body as a recipient of salvation needed to be trained and subdued, so that movements and gestures for prayer reflected European bodies rather than African ones. Orderly bodies were closer to holiness and orderly theological assertions were certainly part of a God that revealed himself through the exact and orderly celebration of the sacraments.

Kabasele Lumbala's presupposition of diversity provides a complete antithesis of what a pre-Vatican II Church and theology had been. Theological *dicta* came from assumed truths that were to be explained and extended, not from the experience of God's revelation in the contemporary world through a particular tradition. For Kabasele Lumbala the celebration of rites in an African culture provides diversity according to a particular context. In his words, 'the remote *Deus ex machina* perched on a remote summit has come down and become our partner in a new covenant'.[54]

Sacraments and Sacramentals

Within his work Kabasele Lumbala develops an ethnography, a descriptive narrative of African rites that were developed after the liturgical encouragement of the Second Vatican Council. In his thought, this chain of liturgical experiments becomes the basis for theological reflection on faith and culture. The movement between textual rites and social developments provides an ongoing dynamic in theology that mediates the usual text = liturgy, or the liberation theology paradigm action = theology.

In that *via media* role, the theology of inculturation becomes central to the experimentation on rites, as particular symbols, gestures and movements have to be connected with diverse theological understandings related to the celebration of the sacraments. Thus, social life = spiritual life, social action = liturgical rites, and theology of culture

= theology of inculturation. Rites created for a particular celebration of the sacraments or created for a particular cultural celebration of a moment of life depend on a dynamic and positive opposition between textual and contextual elements. Those elements are the Roman liturgical texts, particular African gestures and actions, and the theological reflection that mediates between possible opposition in local understandings of faith and culture.

Therefore the theology of inculturation in Kabasele Lumbala requires the centrality of the sacraments attached to Catholic theology, and also the experience of the multicultural by a universal Church that does not describe herself as English, Scottish, Welsh, Congolese or Rwandan. As a condition of theological multiculturalism, the theological reflection on inculturation cannot be associated with a generative theology that begets liturgical rites, but it can be associated with a theology of the *via media*, a middle way of reflection between text and context, between faith and culture. This *via media* has provided a significant mediation between those who have suggested that there is nothing African about Christian theology, and those European missionaries who have suggested that African indigenous discourses and actions can be fully associated with Christian theology. For the latter, even indigenous ways of praying should be better known 'so that they can provide material for a creative African Christian liturgy'.[55]

In the African communities as well as within the global Roman Catholic Church, the whole body of the Church through the localized community shapes her life through the communal celebration of the seven sacraments. Since the Middle Ages, the sacraments have been baptism, confirmation and Eucharist (sacraments of initiation), reconciliation, marriage, anointing of the sick and ordination. Thus, in order to conduct those liturgical celebrations texts from the Roman Missal and the Roman Sacramental are used, with the incorporation of contextual and cultural elements associated with life in Africa. Moreover, through the experimental incorporation of some elements and the exclusion of others, an ongoing reflection on faith and culture within the Roman Catholic tradition is further sustained and increased.

Such theological reflection on the inculturation of the sacraments is also complemented by the use of material objects and blessings outside the liturgical celebration of the sacraments that help the sanctification of spaces and ordinary moments in African life, through the so-called *sacramentals*.[56] Within those sacramentals the presence of God is signified by the use of cultural elements in order to sanctify human activities and to allow God's presence in activities such as harvesting, or the rejection of evil spirits, or the sanctification of daily activities.

Through the use of sacramentals and within the celebration of the sacraments, Christians in Africa do not reject African traditions; however, they correct their trajectory, illumined by Christ and his message. Thus, in the theology of Kabasele Lumbala 'Christ and the history of salvation become the "pole of harmonization" in a world that continues to be understood as dual and marked by diverse participations and mediations shared by ancestors, human beings, animals, vegetables, and seemingly inanimate objects'.[57]

For example, blessings as means of sanctification have been widely used in connection with cultural understandings of kinship and kingship relations within groups and clans. In particular, the blessing of fields has traditionally been associated with the separation of fields from any possibility of infertility and any social division that could lead to death.[58] In developing a Christian ritual for the blessings of fields in parts of Africa it is assumed that a traditional social activity can be given a further theological understanding. Such understanding arises out of the fact that through a blessing on the fields, a communal invocation of God's grace is requested on those associated with a particular field. Within such invocation, the ultimate purpose of the blessing is for those who take part in that liturgical celebration to remain open to the grace of God and to realize their human destiny, which is life with God.

In one of those blessings, Christians bring to the church soil from their fields and some of the seeds to be used for planting. The priest welcomes those Christians at the entrance to the church, liturgically vested and carrying holy water. He asks those coming for the blessing to deposit the soil in one pot and the seeds in another pot. The priest blesses the soil by asking that it may be free from accidents, dangers, thorns or injuries through the use of tools. He blesses the seeds, asking that they may produce a hundred-fold, before sprinkling both soil and seeds with holy water. The priest requests plenty of rain and sunshine and the proper conditions for a good crop that will sustain God's people. After such blessings the pots are moved in procession to the foot of the altar where they are deposited. Psalm 50 is sung and the sign of peace is exchanged. Thereafter the celebration of the Eucharist continues as usual.

The Christian and indigenous African traditions are united in this example, as for Africans to bring some soil from the fields is to bring an entire field to the Church, to bring some seeds is to have brought all the available planting seeds for the Church to bless. However, within the Christian liturgy it is proclaimed and it is accepted that God is the one who makes things grow and he is the one who produces a plentiful harvest. The readings for such occasion proclaim such truths (Gen. 1.27–31; Ps. 126; Jn 12.23–6).

In other regions such as Kasai (Democratic Republic of Congo), the month of February marks the start of the season in which people collect caterpillars from the wooded savanna. Deaths can occur as caterpillar collectors can be beaten by snakes or other poisonous insects, so a blessing for those going out is suggested by Kabasele Lumbala. In this case, not only is there a need to mark the different seasons through liturgical moments, but also the physical change from caterpillar to butterfly can be used to symbolize changes and conversion in the life of a Christian. Thus, an entrance song during the Eucharist and blessing can be chosen with a theme of conversion. Readings that speak of the fruits of Easter and the conversion of Jesus' disciples (e.g. Acts 2.37–47) or the signs of the times (e.g. Luke 21.29–33) follow. A homily after the Gospel follows, trying to focus participants on the change from caterpillars into butterflies and the theme of Christian conversion. The prayers of the faithful focus attention on those who will be gathering caterpillars for community consumption, their generosity and their safety followed by a blessing on them and on a branch with caterpillars. It is through the caterpillars that the glory of God in his creation shines and makes human beings praise God through the offerings and the liturgy of the Eucharist that follows.

Theological Continuities and Cultural Fragmentations

As particular blessings are used for particular seasons and times of the year, the cultural allegory of an inculturated theology develops cultural elements in Africa in the same way that the people of Israel did throughout their own history. The Israelites assumed cultural elements from the lands they passed on their way to the promised land or from the lands that they lived in during periods of their history, such as the Babylonian exile.

Through his *via media* and his theological analysis Kabasele Lumbala's theology has become central to the development of a contemporary theology of inculturation in Africa. His own brand of African theology is centred on the liturgical rites of a particular Christian tradition and on the person of Christ: scripture and tradition as centres of community have provided continuity within the Roman Catholic tradition. Kabasele Lumbala's theological achievement is to centre theological reflection from within Africa in the creative power of liturgical rites. He has focused his theological reflection particularly on those rites that have managed to incorporate contemporary cultural elements not as memories or texts from the past, but as challenging elements with God-given grace and salvific effect within a larger and universal Christian tradition.

The theology of inculturation and those involved in it, including Kabasele Lumbala, have continued to fulfil an important obligation for African theologians, as outlined by Bishop T. Tshibangu in the 1977 meeting of African theologians. He addressed them saying,

> They [African theologians] cannot live as beings apart because they must bear responsibility for their own personal destiny and that of others. They must be involved in their community and their social participation must be as active as possible.[59]

Those conditions are certainly the basis for Kabasele Lumbala's theology of liturgical inculturation. Further, it is through their search for Christ as the centre of African Christianity that a process of ordering has started. Such effort can be compared to the systematic reflection by Jon Sobrino and Leonardo Boff in Latin American theology, in which issues of methodology and criticism of methodology were settled by the publication of theological writings on the person of Christ. If Latin American Christologies aimed at a social context of liberation, African Christologies cannot be deemed less elaborate than in Latin America, but they can be described as inculturated Christologies that seem more elaborate and stronger than in Latin America.

It is after all, Christ's centrality that can connect all bodies of contextual theology within the contemporary world, and therefore any attempt to contextualize the person of Christ in Africa opens fresh ways of Christological reflections at a wider level. So far, African Christian theology has developed a clear theological methodology through which Christian beliefs and doctrines have been thought afresh within the social and religious context of Africa. Within such systematic theological explorations, the spiritual African world of the ancestors has been used in order to explore the place of Christ, his life and resurrection within a wider African context.

The centrality of Christ as the primordial ancestor relates to an African spiritual world that finally meets and celebrates together in the liturgy, honouring once again the memory of Christ and the ancestors through the Eucharist. The challenges of such theological reflection and sacramental action provide a further theological ordering still to be developed, always in a process of change as it is the case of all contextual African theology. What about the Rwandan genocide within all these events? This is the subject of the following chapter.

Notes

1 Ghana (Gold Coast) became independent in 1955, Tanzania in 1961, Kenya in 1963.

2 John Parratt, 1987, 'Introduction', in John Parratt (ed.), *A Reader in African Christian Theology*, London: SPCK, p. 4.

3 John Mbiti, 1979, 'The Biblical Basis for Present Trends in African Theology', in Kofi Appiah-Kubi and Sergio Torres (eds), *African Theology en Route: Papers from the Pan-African Conference of Third World Theologians*, December 17–23, 1977, Accra, Ghana, Maryknoll, NY: Orbis, p. 84.

4 V.Y. Mudimbe, 1988, *The Invention of Africa: Gnosis, Philosophy and the Order of Knowledge*, Bloomington and Indianapolis: Indiana University Press and London: James Currey, p. ix. *Gnosis* in a more general way has also been used in the study of particular religious movement, Jamaa, and their transmission of knowledge, see Johannes Fabian, 1971, *Jamaa: A Charismatic Movement in Katanga*, Evanston, IL: Northwestern University Press and 1994, 'Jamaa: A Charismatic Movement Revisited', in Thomas D. Blakely, Walter E. A. van Beek and Dennis L. Thomson (eds), *Religion in Africa: Experience and Expression*, London: James Currey and Portsmouth, NH: Heinemann. The Jamaa movement was founded by the Belgian missionary Placide Tempels and it is probably the first attempt at an African Christianity with its proper theological system and narrative.

5 O. Bimwenyi, 1981, *Discours Théologique Négro-Africain: Problèmes de Fondements*, Paris: Présence Africaine, in Mudimbe, *Invention*, p. 46.

6 G. W. F. Hegel, 1955, *Sämtliche Werke*, ed. J. Hoffmeister, Hamburg: F. Meiner, p. 167.

7 Here I borrow and I follow Enrique Dussel's Frankfurt Lectures, whose introduction is reproduced as 'Eurocentrism and Modernity (Introduction to the Frankfurt Lectures)', in John Beverley, José Oviedo and Michael Aronna (eds), 1995, *The Postmodernism Debate in Latin America*, Durham and London: Duke University Press, pp. 65–76.

8 Hegel, 'Lectures', in *Werke*, p. 243.

9 Hegel, 'Lectures', in *Werke*, p. 212.

10 Hegel, 'Lectures', in *Werke*, pp. 231–4.

11 Rosino Gibellini, 1994, 'Introduction: African Theologians Wonder . . . And Make Some Proposals', in R. Gibellini (ed.), *Paths of African Theology*, London: SCM Press, pp. 1–5, Parratt, 'Introduction', p. 1, Robert J. Schreiter, 1992, 'Introduction: Jesus Christ in Africa Today', in R. J. Schreiter (ed.), *Faces of Jesus in Africa*, London: SCM Press, p. x.

12 Mudimbe, *Invention*, p. 187.

13 M. Foucault as evaluated by Mudimbe, *Invention*, p. 188.

14 M. de Certeau, 1982, *La Fable Mystique*, Paris: Gallimard, p. 227.

15 Ngindu Mushete, 'The History of Theology in Africa: From Polemics to Critical Irenics', in Appiah-Kubi and Torres (eds), *African Theology*, p. 32.

16 *La Philosophie bantoue*, Elisabethville: Lovania, 1945, Paris: Présence Africaine 1949, English translation *Bantu Philosophy*, Paris: Présence Africaine, 1959.

17 'Final Communiqué', Pan African Conference of Third World Theologians, December 17–23, 1977, Accra, Ghana, in Appiah-Kubi and Torres (eds), *African Theology*, p. 195.

18 'Preface', in Appiah-Kubi and Torres (eds), *African Theology*, p. viii.

19 'Opening Address', in Appiah-Kubi and Torres (eds), *African Theology*, p. 8.

20 Ngindu Mushete, 'The History', p. 29.

21 'African Report', in K.C. Abrahams (ed.), 1990, *Third World Theologies: Commonalities and Divergences*, Papers and Reflections from the Second General Assembly of the Ecumenical Association of Third World Theologians, December, 1986, Oaxtepec, Mexico, Maryknoll, NY: Orbis, p. 49; also Mbiti, 'Biblical Basis', and Kwesi A. Dickson, 'Continuity and Discontinuity Between the Old Testament and African Life and Thought', in Appiah-Kubi and Torres (eds), *African Theology*, pp. 95–108.

22 Sergio Torres, 1979, 'Opening Address', in Appiah-Kubi and Torres (eds), *African Theology*, p. 5. Nevertheless, the theme of the poor and the oppressed within African readings of the Bible has not been as prominent as in Latin America. However, African theologians such as Jean-Marc Éla have explored the political commitment of African theologians outside the South African context.

23 'Final Communiqué', in Appiah-Kubi and Torres (eds), *African Theology*, p. 190.

24 'Final Communiqué', in Appiah-Kubi and Torres (eds), *African Theology*, p. 193.

25 Ogbu U. Kalu, 1979, 'Church Presence in Africa', in Appiah-Kubi and Torres (eds), *African Theology*, pp. 13–14.

26 'African Report', in Abrahams (ed.), *Third World*, p. 51.

27 Ogbu U. Kalu, 1979, 'Church Presence in Africa: A Historical Analysis of the Evangelization Process', in Appiah-Kubi and Torres (eds), *African Theology*, p. 15.

28 Ogbu U. Kalu in Appiah-Kubi and Torres (eds), *African Theology*, p. 16.

29 Gwinyai H. Muzorewa, 1985, *The Origins and Development of African Theology*, Maryknoll, NY: Orbis, p. 17.

30 Mercy Amba Oduyoye, 1979, 'The Value of African Religious Beliefs and Practices for Christian Theology', in Appiah-Kubi and Torres (eds), *African Theology*, p. 111.

31 Gwinyai H. Muzarewa, *Origins*, p. 78.

32 E. W. Fashole-Luke, 1975, 'The Quest for an African Christian Theology', *The Ecumenical Review*, 27 July 1975, pp. 259–69.

33 John Mbiti, 1976, 'Some Currents of African Theology', in J. Mbiti (ed.), *African and Asian Contributions to Contemporary Theology: Report*, Geneva: Bossey, pp. 6–17.

34 John K. Agbeti, 'African Theology: What It Is', *Presence* 5, pp. 5–8.

35 Kwesi Dickson and Paul Ellingworth (eds), 1971, *Biblical Revelation and African Beliefs*, Maryknoll, NY: Orbis, p. 180.

36 Schreiter, 'Introduction: Jesus Christ in Africa Today', p. ix.

37 Charles Nyamiti, a Catholic priest from Tanzania, studied in Europe and has taught systematic theology at the Catholic University of Eastern Africa

(CUEA), formerly the Catholic Higher Institute of East Africa (CHIEA) in Nairobi, Kenya.

38 Mika Vähäkangas, 1999, *In Search of Foundations for African Catholicism: Charles Nyamiti's Theological Methodology*, Leiden: Koninklijke Brill.

39 François Kabasele Lumbala, 1998, *Celebrating Jesus Christ in Africa: Liturgy and Inculturation*, Maryknoll, NY: Orbis.

40 F. Kabasele Lumbala, 1987, 'Sin, Confession and Reconciliation in Africa', in Mary Collins and David Power (eds), *The Fate of Confession* (*Concilium* 190), Edinburgh: T&T Clark, pp. 74–81 and 1995, 'Christians and Muslims in Africa', in Louis-Marie Chauvet and François Kabasele Lumbala (eds), 1995, *Liturgy and the Body* (*Concilium* 1995/3), London: SCM Press, Maryknoll: Orbis, pp. 64–70. Other works in French include *Pâques africaines d'aujourd'hui*, Paris: Desclée, 1989, *Symbolique bantu et symbolique chrétienne: Rencontre dans la liturgie*, Kinshasa, 1991, *Alliances avec le Christ en Afrique: Inculturation des rites religieux au Zaïre*, Paris: Karthala, 1994 and *Liturgies africaines: L'enjeu culturel, ecclésial et théologique*, Kinshasa: Ed. Facultés de Théologie, 1996.

41 V. Mulago, 1965, *Un visage africain du christianisme*, Paris: Présence Africaine and 1979, *Simbolismo Religioso Africano: Estudio Comparativo con el Sacramentalismo Cristiano*, Madrid: BAC.

42 Jean-Marc Éla, 1994, 'Christianity and Liberation in Africa', in Rosino Gibellini (ed.), *Paths of African Theology*, London: SCM Press, p. 137. Cf. 1986, *African Cry*, Maryknoll, NY: Orbis and 1988, *My Faith as an African*, Maryknoll, NY, Orbis and London: Geoffrey Chapman.

43 See *The Kairos Document: Challenge to the Church*, London: CIIR, 1986, Simon S. Maimela, 1981, 'Man in White Theology', *Journal of Theology for Southern Africa* 36, pp. 30–41 and 'Being a Christian in South Africa', in Giuseppe Alberigo and Alphonse Ngindu Mushete (eds), 1992, *Towards the African Synod* (*Concilium* 1992/1), London: SCM Press, pp. 52–8, also Albert Nolan, 1988, *God in South Africa: The Challenge of the Gospel*, London: CIIR and Charles Villa-Vicencio (ed.), 1988, *Theology and Violence: The South African Debate*, Grand Rapids, MI: Eerdmans.

44 See Simon S. Maimela, 1987, *Proclaim Freedom to My People*, Johannesburg: Skotaville Publishers and 1994, 'Black Theology of Liberation', in Gibellini (ed.), *Paths of African Theology*, pp. 182–95.

45 F. Kabasele Lumbala, 1994, 'Africans Celebrate Jesus Christ', in Gibellini (ed.), *Paths of African Theology*, p. 79, cf. 'L'au-delà des modèles', in François Kabasele, Joseph Doré and René Luneau (eds), 1988, *Chemins de la christologie africaine*, Paris: Desclée.

46 Kabasele Lumbala, 'Africans Celebrate Jesus Christ', p. 81.

47 Kabasele Lumbala, *Celebrating*, p. 110.

48 F. Kabasele Lumbala, 1992, 'Christ as Chief' and 'Christ as Ancestor and Elder Brother', in Schreiter (ed.), *Faces of Jesus in Africa*, pp. 103–15, 116–27.

49 Theologians in Latin America have also pointed out the difficulties of an over-imposition of Western culture through Christianity, a culture 'marked by the logocentrism and individualism of the Greek tradition'. Thus, 'the official liturgy of the church is strongly marked by the Western experience of a perceived superiority of spirit to matter, a mistrust of the body and its passions, and

great restraint in its symbolic expression'; see Leonardo Boff, 1992, *Good News to the Poor: A New Evangelization*, Tunbridge Wells: Burns & Oates, p. 42.

50 Kabasele Lumbala, *Celebrating*, p. 3.

51 Kabasele Lumbala, *Celebrating*, p. 5.

52 F. Kabasele Lumbala, 1994, *Alliances avec le Christ en Afrique: Inculturation des rites religieux au Zaïre*, Paris: Karthala.

53 Kabasele Lumbala, *Celebrating*, p. 115.

54 Kabasele Lumbala, *Celebrating*, p. 110.

55 Aylward Shorter, 'Prayer in African Cultural Tradition', in Teresa Okure, Paul van Thiel et al. (eds), *32 Articles Evaluating Inculturation of Christianity in Africa*, Eldoret, Kenya: AMECEA Gaba Publications, Spearhead 112–114, p. 251. This paper was originally published in the *African Ecclesial Review* 14/1, 1972, pp. 11–7.

56 'Sacramentals are instituted for the sanctification of certain ministries of the Church, certain states of life, a great variety of circumstances in Christian life, and the use of many things useful to man. In accordance with bishop's pastoral decisions, they can also respond to the needs, culture and special history of the Christian people of a particular region or time', *Catechism of the Catholic Church* § 1668, London: Geoffrey Chapman, 1994. See also Documents of the Second Vatican Council, e.g. Instruction on the Proper Implementation of the Constitution on the Sacred Liturgy, *Inter Oecumenici* § 6, 34; The Constitution on the Sacred Liturgy, *Sacrosanctum Concilium* § 60–3, 79; and Instruction on Music in the Liturgy, *Musicam Sacram* § 45.

57 Kabasele Lumbala, *Celebrating*, p. 96.

58 Kabasele Lumbala, *Celebrating*, pp. 102–3.

59 Bishop T. Tshibangu (Zaire), 1979, 'The Task of African Theologians' in Appiah-Kubi and Torres (eds), *African Theology*, p. 75.

5

Theological Liberation and Weak Thought

The attempts at a construction of an African theology based on a communion with the ancestors, as outlined in the previous chapter, intended to challenge the universal paradigm of a European theology based on philosophical paradigms.[1] However, the events of Rwanda made the contra-colonial and post-colonial discourse somehow a matter of the past because the oppressors of the poor and the makers of victims in Africa were African themselves within Rwanda.[2] Within that context of a possible hermeneutics of suspicion an African theology of post-colonialism could fall into the trap of becoming once again a mechanism of universalism without being challenged. That is not the case but it is always a dangerous possibility. Thus, inculturation could worry the Vatican or the liturgists that advocate a universalism of liturgical symbols; however, it has not provided the possibilities of avoiding the suffering of millions of Africans who live in poverty, misery and oppression. In the summary provided by the Tanzanian theologian Laurenti Magesa:

> It is rather ironical and difficult to explain the fact that as the church in Africa is today in the midst of the transition from a predominantly missionary-structured and -oriented church to an African based one, it at the same time seems to be engulfed by a fortress-like mood.[3]

Here I am very conscious that the possibility of liturgical and symbolic creativity by a particular theological school, local church or community helps to develop the spirit of liberation from colonialism.[4] Nevertheless, the experience of Rwanda and Zimbabwe points to a renewed urgency in the rethinking of a theological model that can provide the possible ground for a full human liberation, that is within the liturgy and doctrine as well as within the sociopolitical contexts in which any liturgy is celebrated. Further, there is a necessity to respond to these contexts of poverty and oppression by challenging new universalisms that arise not any longer out of a colonial machinery but out of the ongoing strong centrality of a systematic theology that bases itself on a strong philosophical universalism that after all is based on European thought, rationality, a unified ontology. This pseudo-Platonism of ideas has also made Europe into a decreasing milieu for the work of the Spirit and a continent in which the decreasing numbers of practising faithful suggest that the practice of religion has become detached from the urgency of daily life and the human projects of communities. Those who seek alternative spiritualities in Europe have seen the churches not as creative and supportive of diversity but as legalistic instruments of ethics and morals as central to the human communication between the struggling human and the divine. The daily communication between people and their God has been ultimately corroded by this legalistic vision and the contemplation that leads to action by individual Christians and their communities needs to be restored if Christianity as a European mode of existence is to remain a possibility.[5]

European and Non-European Thought

This chapter deals with possible theological elements central to a liberation theology that can deal with 'the death of God', 'the absence of God' and the central commandment to love God and neighbour. It has been a failure, and a necessary device, for liberation theology not to engage too closely in dialogue with European theology or European thought. It has been a lack of Christianity whereby there has been an absence of God and an absence of spiritual values, particularly within the African elites. It is sadly towards the African elites that have actually managed to leave poverty and under-development that the churches looked with enthusiasm and hope at the time of independence. It is partly due to the African elites that African democracies have been tainted with so much corruption and greed; the case of Zimbabwe is only one recent example.

Indeed, the first generation of theologians of liberation, with the exception of the Argentinean Enrique Dussel, rejected the possibility of dealing with analytical philosophy and they concentrated their theological project, as the African theologians have done, on a fresh and liberating reading of the biblical text.[6] Of course, for those who considered Marxism as an analytical philosophy, liberation theologians engaged very closely with Latin American Marxists and with the possibilities of social analysis through the use of historical materialism.[7] If I may be controversial for some in my attempt to engage with European philosophy, it must be remembered that the era of disengagement with other theologies (and philosophies) has been disrupted and somehow buried by the chronology of the 1994 Rwandan genocide, the ethnic cleansing in the Balkans, the plane attacks on New York and Washington DC on 9/11 and the consequent 'war on terror', the rendition flights and the torture and imprisonment of enemies of the United States in the prison camp of Guantánamo Bay (Cuba). These realities of neo-colonialism and globalization are common to all, because they are a clear expression of a dehumanization and the mechanization of pain, suffering and the disrespect for the dignity of any human being, commonly united by the same rights and the same dignity of being God's creation. Caryn Riswold argued before the 2008 US presidential elections that what the United States needed was 'a leader who does not exercise unilateral power and make decisions based on ideology and personal preference', and what liberation theology needs is an open search for the realities of globalization and a direct critical engagement with the ideas that reflect God's preferential option for the poor, on the one hand, and those ideas that prevent the realization of this utopian vision and divine realization on the other.[8]

I would argue, without apologies, that this is the time to regain a philosophical as well as a sociopolitical engagement with those elites and those intellectuals who are still functioning within an ontological and supra-structured world of ideas that seems to have more credibility than ideas related to the poor. Those ontological and metaphysical ideas have been challenged and confronted by postmodernity; however, in only few cases have those ideas been assumed as part of the role of the churches and the role of liberation theology. I follow the challenging lead of Iván Petrella, when he outlines a possible new way of doing liberation theology and writes:

> Perhaps the task is that of disentangling the 'liberation' from the 'theology' in liberation theology. To work in liberation theology today could mean to work outside it, by finding ways the epistemological and practical-moral elements can infiltrate, subvert and transform other bodies of knowledge. Here the liberation theologian need not carry the label of 'theologian' and works best under a different disciplinary guise.[9]

I attempt to open avenues of theological exploration, helped by the refreshing new dialogues between a Roman Catholic philosopher, the Italian Gianni Vattimo, and the north American philosopher Richard

Rorty, whose philosophical edifice has influenced Western thought but with whom the Argentinean Enrique Dussel engaged in dialogue in his book *The Underside of Modernity: Ricoeur, Apel, Taylor and the Philosophy of Liberation.*[10] Thus, this chapter engages ideas of the previous two sections with the philosophical thought and the work on religion by the Italian Gianni Vattimo who in 2007 wrote in his *The Future of Religion* that the basis of all religion, and a practice that precedes theology, is love.[11] This was an unexpected conclusion to a dialogue with Richard Rorty that has shocked some European thinkers and has enhanced liberation theology since Rwanda. Theology is no longer, even for some Europeans, a rational enterprise or apologetic, but an act of hermeneutical inscription of God's love. By weakening ontology and platonic thought Vattimo has revived the idea that human beings have duties towards God, as it was before the Enlightenment, a period in which reason dominated the human duties that created a false dichotomy between an 'Age of Faith' and an 'Age of Reason' while the contemporary conversation between Rorty and Vattimo, witnessed by Santiago Zabala, assumes the position that humanity has entered the 'Age of Interpretation'.[12]

Liberation and Interpretation

In his ethical and philosophical work Enrique Dussel had already questioned the possibility of platonic thought and an overriding fixed ontology, of matter and of God.[13] A new Latin American way of thinking had been described by Dussel as creative, historical, concrete, committed, asystematic, prophetic and anguished.[14] Thus, philosophy becomes for Dussel a liberating project when the philosopher is in union with a historical subject so that 'concrete articulation from within a people is a *conditio sine qua non* for the philosophizing of liberation' and the actualization of that project can mean for the philosopher 'losing one's freedom in prison, enduring the pain of torture, losing a professorship at a university, and perhaps being killed, given the situation in Latin America'.[15]

In the theological and sociopolitical context of the twentieth century, philosophical vulnerability was possible and desirable; however, the fall of the Berlin Wall suggested the possibility of economic progress through unification rather than through diversity. The interpretation of a possible liberation as action was replaced by reason and by the reasonable expectation that once political change arose progress, stability, freedom and creativity would arise. That never happened and genocide became once again a possibility in the Balkans with new questions and new challenges for a liberating philosophy that continued exploring a different world but within a complete overriding paradigm of increasing consumerism and globalization.

After the collapse of the Berlin Wall the postmodern condition had suggested the possibility of the end of metanarratives, but the advent of a unified effort to develop Eastern Europe and other parts of the world brought a new metanarrative into play: the neo-colonial paradigm of globalization. It is at this moment that the 'age of faith' and the 'age of reason' became obsolete because neither secularization nor the challenges to science made any difference to a world dominated by the United States and the metanarratives of economic prosperity and the ontology of a divine being that became closely linked with economic progress; economic blessings became associated with divine intervention and economic success was attributed to a divine will to exclude others who didn't agree with either 'the clash of civilizations' or the possibility of the end of a separation between the public role of religion and politics in the United States. President George W. Bush and Prime Minister Tony Blair used their own faith understanding to suggest that a new 'liberation' of Iraq from dictator Saddam Hussein in 2003 was not only necessary but by implication willed by God and the values of Western civilization.

It is within this context that the life-long philosophical work of Gianni Vattimo became a challenge to the dying humanism of a 'war in terror' by suggesting that a new 'age of interpretation' became the language of all, the language of those who had challenged the actual possibilities of theism and atheism such as Richard Rorty. For Vattimo argues, following Heidegger in section 1 of *Being and Time*, that 'knowledge is always interpretation and nothing but this', and that 'interpretation is the only *fact* of which we can speak'.[16] If Nietzsche introduces the possibility of nihilism and Heidegger the end of metaphysics by letting events speak, Lyotard and his end of metanarratives overlooked the possibility that the narratives still existed after being denied and needed to be looked at once again because the condition of postmodernity did not provide a state of truth after the negation of the meta-truths. It is here that Vattimo argues strongly for a more mainstream understanding of Heidegger's sense of the end of metaphysics in the following words:

> we are called upon to grasp a guiding thread that we can use in order to project its further development; that is, to remain inside it as interpreters rather than as objective recorders of facts.[17]

Vattimo remains within 'a guiding threat' and explores the possibility of human creativity vis-à-vis the human experience of God because it provides limits to any ontological exploration that in the past was deemed as normative. The realization that an event has something to say to humanity in search of meaning (in Vattimo's words 'to let the event speak') has a clear repercussion:

> this event comprises the end of Eurocentrism, the critique of ideology, the dissolution of the evidentness of consciousness through psychoanalysis, the explicit pluralisation of the agencies of information, the mass media.[18]

Thus, in my own reading of Vattimo, any event is meaningful by itself regardless of the possibility that for the witness the event could be nihilistic and somehow devoid of interpretation. For it is possible to argue with Vattimo that the role of Christianity has been changed within contemporary society and Christianity cannot only be perceived as meaningful through the utopian connection between the practices of Christianity and public society. Truth lies not within the ontological definitions or the philosophical negations of particular truths but within the historical event and subject, within what liberation theology called 'the first moment' or in the definition by Jung Mo Sung 'the experience of ethical indignation'.[19]

This is where Vattimo's arguments connect with liberation theology. If Christianity seems to be nihilistic and empty, it is only because it has responded as an anti-metaphysical response to the dreams of an ontological way of appreciating the world that has made human beings prisoners of platonic worlds in which human beings do not find their identity any longer. Vattimo's response to this absence of a humane and democratic society relates to his own search and to his own experience of serving within the contemporary world of European politics. However, within his theoretical development of a Christian existence after the end of theism and atheism he develops a third possibility that does not engage with the previous ontological realities but moves into a new understanding of the possibilities of a Christianity freed from an ontological and rational explanation for all. He writes:

> There is a third possibility between, on the one hand, the metaphysical demonstration of the truth of Christianity (the *preambula fidei* and the historical veracity of the resurrection) and, on the other, its falseness with respect to scientific reason (entailing the quasi-naturalistic acceptance of the differences among individuals,

cultures, and societies): Christianity as a historical message of salvation.[20]

It is interesting that, after a life full of doubt about the Church and Christianity, Vattimo argued for the possibility of a historicity within life as a Christian, asserting that 'if I were not a Christian I would probably be a metaphysician'.[21] For in Vattimo's understanding and practice, belief is always in the making and is not a given; for belief and the assertion of belief in God is no more than a personal assertion of a plausibility. He writes: 'well, I believe that I believe'.[22] In dialogue with a non-believer such as Richard Rorty, Vattimo expressed their absolute similarity in philosophy but the fact that Vattimo's sense of event and being was framed daily by the reading of the biblical text and by the fact that the text didn't support ontology but the history of a living God. For Rorty, 1 Corinthians 13 and the centrality of love, as kind, patient and enduring all, can unite believers and unbelievers. However, in his words: 'the difference between these two sorts of people is that between unjustifiable gratitude and unjustifiable hope'.[23]

It is within that 'age of hermeneutics' that Vattimo returns to the most traditional of meanings of hermeneutics, that reading and interpretation of a message, an event for a particular human being in search of identity and being. It is also within that ongoing hermeneutics that Vattimo took part in the world of active politics and questioned, as Dussel did, the possibility of understanding wisdom or philosophy without understanding the actions of human beings within the real world and particularly within the world of contemporary politics. Thus, Dussel refers to how liberation theologians used Marxism, arguing that 'liberation theology uses a *certain* Marxism in a *certain way* – never in such a way as to be incompatible with the foundations of the faith'.[24]

The Age of Hermeneutics and Politics

One of the central chores of understanding for a dialogue between Third World theologies of the liberationist kind and European thought has never been a particular theoretical understanding or the preference for a particular theological or philosophical paradigm. In the metaphor used by Clodovis Boff:

> Liberation theology is like a tree. If you see only professional theologians, you are looking only at the branches. You are missing the trunk, which is the reflection of the pastors and other ministers, and

> you are certainly missing all the roots, which are beneath the surface of the soil and maintain the entire tree, trunk and branches alike.[25]

In the case of Vattimo the possible comparison of praxis and action for the socially marginalized and liberation theology's preferential option for the poor and the marginalized connect through Vattimo's own historical journey. As in the case of Latin American liberationists Vattimo's journey started as a committed Christian, a Roman Catholic, who developed his interests in the world, and his social, religious and political interests through the church. He studied philosophy in order to continue taking part in that blend of human interests. In his own words, 'I wanted to contribute to the formation of a new Christian humanism, which would be free from liberal individualism and from collective and deterministic Marxism'.[26] After reading Jacques Maritain on his intellectual youth he became engrossed with the critique of modernity by Nietzsche and Heidegger who were not only anti-modern but anti-Christian.[27]

It was through a hermeneutics of the actual human being in a historical perspective and the impossibility of denying the essence of God that Vattimo returned to the Christian faith. If atheists had understood Nietzsche's work as denying the existence of God, Vattimo's work with the original sources argued that, in the interpretation of both thinkers, Nietzsche and Heidegger, commentators had not understood the fact that the philosophers' assertions were only interpretations and that the negation of God had not been logically proven. Thus, 'the decline of metaphysics as a systematic philosophy, which conferred a consistent, unified, and rigorously grounded representation of the stable structures of Being, has made the philosophical denial of God's existence impossible'.[28] For Vattimo, the biblical text becomes credible after modernity because it can be studied and critically assessed as historically constructed and because at the end supports the idea of God as *verbum*, as the Word who becomes incarnate, thus weakening any rational and ontological understanding of an essence with no connection with his history, event or being. With modernity and post-modernity, a Western God linked to a European conception of society and the state has been weakened to the point that the *verbum* cannot be a prisoner of reason or of medieval faith but continues a process of historical connection with events and beings who provide diversity and who engage with a *verbum* who is as much part of the history and event of the Cross and does not exist as an essence of wisdom without any link to human events.

However, the reclaiming of Christianity without colonialism and

Eurocentrism, that is, with a sense that all societies and human beings are in a linear progression and evolution towards European societies, can only take place if Christianity 'recovers its profound solidarity with the destiny of modernization'.[29] Vattimo's engagement with this modernization occurs in his active participation in European politics; after joining the Italian Communists he served as a member of the European Parliament from 1999 to 2004 under the umbrella of the Party of European Socialists. It is this particular action that makes him in my opinion connect once again with a God who cannot be dead while political and social action continue and active charity is dispensed. For this is the intellectual and philosopher who leaves the ivory tower of Turin where he had been full professor since 1969 in order to immerse himself in the complex and difficult politics of the European Union at a time in which the political tendencies of the Italian electorate aim towards the far right and Italy supports the 'war on terror' while Prime Minister Silvio Berlusconi becomes a close ally and even friend of the US President George W. Bush.

Vattimo had been fully involved in the 1992 Italian political crisis in which a police investigation into political parties managed to finish the party of his youth, the Christian Democrats. After the political revolution against bribes that took place in Italy Vattimo took part in the national debate through newspaper columns in *La Stampa* and *L'Unità*, not only criticizing the dissolution of this new political revolution but also challenging the Italian electorate's support for Berlusconi and his House of Liberty Coalition that included the neo-fascist National Alliance of Gianfranco Fini and the xenophobic Northern League of Umberto Bossi.[30] In the European Parliament Vattimo was a member of the Commission of Freedom and Citizens' Rights, Justice and Internal Affairs, the Commission for Culture, Youth, Education, Communication and Sport and the inter-parliamentary delegation from the European Union to China. Vattimo helped to shape the European Union Constitution and contributed to the challenges to Berlusconi by journalists who wanted to highlight accusations against the Italian Prime Minister when he took over the European Union presidency in July 2003.

During those years Vattimo served European politics as a moral and ethical philosopher, who despite the all-embracing structures in politics managed to remind others of the centrality of individual rights and of a political and philosophical project that could emancipate humanity. In the critical summary by Paolo Flores D'Arcais 'the task that Vattimo assigns to philosophy is, in fact, radically political' so that 'philosophy *as* philosophy must be the instrument of *liberation*. Such a liberating and emancipator vocation constitutes – also and above all – the *responsibility* of the philosopher'.[31] This kind of ethical responsibility unites once again Vattimo with Dussel and through Dussel with the first generation of theologians of liberation. But if Dussel made his enterprise to challenge any philosophical ethics devoid of history Vattimo managed to make history a divine ethics. This kind of divine ethics remains a challenging dissolution of a centralized essence by the fact that the God of the Bible becomes complex and historical and Christianity remains a European sectarian movement to be weakened not by discrimination but through the affirmation of the end of metaphysics.

The Politics of Service

The service of a philosopher to politics remains a challenging activity because a philosopher, a seeker of wisdom, is usually associated with a rational determinism that cannot account for the changes and imaginary complexities of party politics. But it is here that Vattimo connects with other contemporary lovers of people and of service such as the President of Paraguay, Fernando Lugo, still a suspended bishop of the Catholic Church, and a person who decided to challenge the kind of traditional politics that serves the politician and the public figure rather than the needs and aspirations of the poor and the marginalized.[32] Lugo and Vattimo decided to make the leap in order to serve while they could have been doing something else: one celebrating the Eucharist with the Christian communities of Paraguay, the other teaching at the University of Turin. It reminds me of the answer that the Nicaraguan poet and priest Ernesto Cardenal gave to those who asked him about his office as Minister for Culture in the Sandinista government that displaced the Nicaraguan dictator Anastasio Somoza in 1979. Cardenal always said that it was very difficult for him to be a government minister because he was a contemplative; he served as a minister because it was for the good of the people while he would have preferred to return to live as a contemplative as he had done in the community of Solentiname before the Nicaraguan revolution.

It is of the essence of the hermeneutics of service to recognize that the politicians involved in Rwanda before and during the 1994 genocide forgot the possibilities and immediacy of service. Oppression and death arrived because the politicians collaborated with a preparation of a social orgy of death, unlike Vattimo, Cardenal and Lugo. The hermeneutics of politics within a postmodern time and within the postmodern condition returns to the basics of charity and love and rejects the possibility of an anti-humanism and the mechanics of death, be it a social death or a hermeneutical death. Thus, Teresa Oñate in her critical engagement with Vattimo and the Christian God has articulated the enormous possibilities of an age of hermeneutics through the following comment:

> Postmodernity, continuing with the emancipation of violence, has to be currently situated in another ontological-rational place: one that goes back to the evangelical (and, consequently, hermeneutical) origins of the Christian spiritual message, assuming them now, transfigured, not as primitive origins at the start of a process, but as symbolic origins that are at the end of the process of liberation, because they are its spiritual sense: that of love, friendship, charity, grace, and forgiveness, as principle-criterion-limit of hermeneutical rationality put in motion.[33]

It is my contention that genocide, ethnic cleansing and all those very dehumanizing crimes arise out of the lack of service, charity and love to others. It is because God is still present; God has not died though he could be considered dead by some. If God were dead some acts of solidarity, love and heroism would not take place. The need planted deep within humans to communicate, and the possibilities of a utopian society, connect human activities, even in the depths of despair, to the moment of the incarnation and the kenosis, the all-giving of Jesus of Nazareth at the cross, where he dies as a criminal for his friends and for the redemption of suffering, pain and all the victims of the powerful and the rich. It is this moment that connects with Vattimo's end of metaphysical principles with Cardenal's aesthetic political activity for the marginalized of Nicaragua and the efforts of Bishop Fernando Lugo of Paraguay to engage in politics for the sake of those he ministered to in a remote Catholic diocese in Paraguay.

The utopian beginnings of liberation theology prepared a challenge at that time to the rich nations by placing the poor and the marginalized at the centre. The context of a globalized world of postmodernity has placed the liberation paradigm outside Christianity and within Christianity at the same time; the heroes of the first generation of liberation theology are coming to the end of their biological lives but a new generation has pointed to further cooperation with the world of economics (Petrella), with new practices in complex human sexuality (Althaus-Reid) and the innate human desire that has created the markets as a challenge to transcendence (Jung Mo Sung). In all of those new challenges for liberation theology there has been a positive assessment of the centrality of the poor and the possibility of learning from the poor, always in a positive tension between the Christian communities and their cooperation with other agents in the world.[34] As I have argued in this chapter those critical efforts by a new generation of liberation theologians would continue bearing the fruits of a 'hermeneutics of suspicion' within a wider engagement with a globalized world.

My argument and dream is very simple. After the Rwandan genocide, the ethnic cleansing that took place in the Balkans and the attacks on New York and Washington, DC on 9/11, liberationists must once again help God's liberation of human beings, God's action in the world through the poor and the marginalized, by engaging their efforts of critical reflection and of sociopolitical action with other humanized agents who remain part of a liberation movement but who do not consider themselves attached to the grassroots of Christian communities in Latin America, Africa or Asia. If previously there were very few partners of liberation in Europe after the processes of secularization and market globalization in the European Union after the fall of the Berlin Wall, the moment has changed. Gianni Vattimo has shown that there are critical thinkers in Europe and indeed North America who can be partners of liberation theologians and *de facto* partners of God's agency as the liberator of the poor, the marginalized and the victims of oppression.[35] There are events that indicate that if a globalized economic power seems to be constructing a world of consumption and false beauty, a movement against the power of the G-8, against poverty, against violence and against dehumanization seems to be growing. Examples of these alliances for liberation of the poor and the oppressed are the meetings of the World Forum on Theology and Liberation (Brazil 2005, 2009) and the meetings of the World Social Forum (Brazil 2003).

Leonardo Boff has argued that there are two central utopias that dominate the contemporary project of liberation in a globalized world in crisis: 'the utopia to safeguard our common home – planet Earth; and the utopia to preserve the human family'.[36] These utopias, I would argue, constitute a globalized project in which all human beings can take part and in which all liberationists, those *de jure* and those *de facto*, can participate. The creation of an alternative project reiterates the possibilities of a theology of the periphery that as I have previously argued becomes in liberationist hermeneutics the central place for God's action. It is here in the refreshed 'age of hermeneutics' outlined by Vattimo that the God who liberates because his essence is to be a liberator can act once again. It is in that variety of the human, religious and common experience that human beings find a common goal with God's agents, that is with the poor and the marginalized. Once again, I must emphasize that theological paradigms and narratives that have stressed the essences of a philosophical and rational God have interpreted God in a Eurocentric manner that has damaged and oppressed many. We are not, as theologians, able to grasp the totality and infinity of God; we can only rejoice in God's plan to become human and in his love for the poor and the marginalized. Wanda Deifelt has put it plainly: the arrogance of theologians, who have then used power and authority to frighten others with their theological schemes, has translated knowledge into sin. In her argument, human arrogance 'reduces speech about God to one cosmovision, to the exclusion of all others, in the name of an absolute'.[37]

It is not surprising that when theological essences are challenged the world of God seems to be more divine, more living, more exciting and the agents of liberation show their happiness through God's happiness and dance and talk and drink wine together. It is that utopia in two acts proclaimed by Leonardo Boff that sets the tone for the possibility of a humanized divinity and for a globalized liberation that was refreshed by the poor of Latin America and has expanded to the poor of Europe and North America. The moment for a divine globalization is here and we must embrace the challenge and the *kairos*. Those who tried before were killed not only in Latin America but also in Africa and Asia. I could think that Gandhi in India proclaimed the same message from his own standpoint of Hinduism. As he wrote:

> And as I know that God is found more often in the lowliest of His creatures than in the high and mighty, I am struggling to reach the status of these. I cannot do so without their service. Hence my passion for the service of the suppressed classes. And as I cannot render this service without entering politics, I find myself in them.[38]

The politics of the Kingdom are more imminent and the field of contemplation and action becomes clearer thanks to Vattimo's weakening of knowledge and the centrality of love as a Christian central mode of action, a mode of action within globalization that certainly unites liberationists throughout movements for utopia and throughout the world religions. It is to the possibilities of a common humanity that I turn in the next chapter. It is symptomatic of the globalized twenty-first century that more recent doctrinal disputes have been centred upon the issue of salvation in other religions, as well as in Christianity. Doctrinal 'truths' related to Christocentric views have provided refreshed prayers for the conversion of the Jews on Good Friday and those theologians who have argued for a closer dialogue with other faiths have come under Vatican scrutiny.[39] However, with armed conflict in Afghanistan and terrorist attacks in Europe led by Muslim fundamentalists, the choice has been political distrust rather than unity in purpose and unity in a common humanity.

In the next chapter, I argue that one of the central trends in liberation theology should continue an engagement, appreciation and collaboration with all world religions, in order to liberate humanity from the anti-values of consumerism and greed that over the centuries have been challenged not only by Christian ethics but also by Buddhism, Hinduism and Islam. If the globalized movements for a better humanity are very close allies to theologians of liberation, members of other world religions are the natural partners in recognizing human beings, with their dignity and rights, as equal; this is the base for the changing of unjust structures and the best prevention of any future genocide. For the *Declaration of the Relation of the Church to Non-Christian Religions* of the Second Vatican Council is very clear when it states that 'there is no basis therefore, either in theory or in practice for any discrimination between individual and individual, or between people and people arising either from human dignity or from the rights which flow from it'.[40] More recently, Claude Geffré has argued that 'while missionary expansion followed the paths of the colonial conquest from the North to the South, we now have to refer to a new impregnation of religious traditions from the East into the Western world'.[41] This timely remark cannot be ignored any longer within theological circles and certainly it cannot be ignored by liberationists. And it is within those Eastern religious traditions that the same common message and way of life that prevents genocide is found, particularly within the central tenets of Buddhism in general and Tibetan Buddhism in particular. The lesson of Rwanda is that genocide arises out of a social discourse that declares people unequal rather than equal and that centres all tenets of human understanding within an ethnic group rather than on a common humanity.

Notes

1 See for example, F. Kabasele Lumbala, 1998, *Celebrating Jesus Christ in Africa: Liturgy and Inculturation*, Maryknoll, NY: Orbis, pp. 41–50.

2 See an analysis of the cruelty by Africans on Africans in John Rucya-

hana with James Riordan, 2007, *The Bishop of Rwanda: Finding Forgiveness Amidst a Pile of Bones*, Nashville, TN: Thomas Nelson.

3 Laurenti Magesa, 2004, *Anatomy of Inculturation: Transforming the Church in Africa*, Maryknoll, NY: Orbis, p. 270.

4 This was the case of the Zairian rite and the liturgical works that preceded the liturgical experimentations in Africa after Vatican II; see for example *Des prêtres noirs s'interrogent*, Paris: Cerf, 1957.

5 For a fuller argument on the relation between contemplation and politics see Mario I. Aguilar, 2008, *Contemplating God, Changing the World*, London: SPCK, pp. 118–34.

6 I am aware here of the nature of liberation theology as a 'second act' and I fully agree with Iván Petrella when he states that he would be unhappy to transfer Richard Rorty's definition of philosophy as 'a kind of writing' to liberation theology; see Iván Petrella, 2007, 'Theology and Liberation: Juan Luis Segundo and Three Takes on Secular Inventiveness', in Marcella Althaus-Reid, Iván Petrella and Luiz Carlos Susin (eds), *Another Possible World*, London: SCM Press, pp. 162–77, at p. 162.

7 Here it is important to reiterate Dussel's analysis: 'liberation theologians unanimously reject dialectical materialism' and 'no liberation theologian accepts the materialism expounded by Frederick Engels in his *Dialectic of Nature*, or of Lenin, Bukharin, or Stalin'; see Enrique D. Dussel, 1993, 'Theology of Liberation and Marxism', in Ignacio Ellacuría SJ and Jon Sobrino SJ (eds), *Mysterium Liberationis: Fundamental Concepts of Liberation Theology*, Maryknoll, NY: Orbis and North Blackburn, Victoria: Collins Dove, pp. 85–102, at p. 87.

8 Caryn D. Riswold, 2007, 'What America Needs in 2008: Educated Problem-Solving and Kitchen Table Values', *Political Theology* 8 (2007/4), pp. 429–41, at p. 434.

9 Iván Petrella, 2008, *Beyond Liberation Theology: A Polemic*, London: SCM Press, p. 150.

10 New York: Humanities Press, 1996, originally published as *Apel, Ricouer, Rorty y la filosofía de la liberación*, Guadalajara, Mexico: Universidad de Guadalajara, 1994.

11 Santiago Zabala (ed.), 2005, *The Future of Religion: Richard Rorty and Gianni Vattimo*, New York: Columbia University Press.

12 Santiago Zabala, 2005, 'Introduction: A Religion without Theists or Atheists', in Zabala (ed.), *The Future of Religion*, pp. 1–27, at p. 4.

13 For an analysis of Dussel's work see Mario I. Aguilar, 2007, *The History and Politics of Latin American Theology*, vol. 1, London: SCM Press, pp. 41–55.

14 Enrique Dussel, 1978, *Ethics and the Theology of Liberation*, Maryknoll, NY: Orbis, pp. 141–2.

15 Enrique Dussel, 2003, *Philosophy of Liberation*, Eugene, OR: Wipf & Stock, p. 190.

16 Gianni Vattimo, 2005, 'The Age of Interpretation', in Zabala (ed.), *The Future of Religion*, pp. 43–54 at p. 44.

17 Vattimo, 'The Age of Interpretation', p. 46.

18 Vattimo, 'The Age of Interpretation', p. 46.

19 Jung Mo Sung, 2005, 'The Human Being as Subject: Defending the

Victims', in Iván Petrella (ed.), *Latin American Liberation Theology: The Next Generation*, Maryknoll, NY: Orbis, pp. 1–19, at p. 4.

20 Vattimo, 'The Age of Interpretation', p. 52.

21 Richard Rorty, Gianni Vattimo and Santiago Zabala, 2005, 'Dialogue: What is Religion's Future after Metaphysics?', in Zabala (ed.), *The Future of Religion*, pp. 55–81, at p. 63.

22 Gianni Vattimo, 2002, *After Christianity*, New York: Columbia University Press, p. 2.

23 Richard Rorty, 2005, 'Anticlericalism and Atheism', in Zabala (ed.), *The Future of Religion*, pp. 29–41, at p. 40.

24 Enrique D. Dussel, 1993, 'Theology of Liberation and Marxism', in Ellacuría and Sobrino (eds), *Mysterium Liberationis Fundamental Concepts of Liberation Theology*, pp. 85–102, at p. 92.

25 Clodovis Boff, 1993, 'Epistemology and Method of the Theology of Liberation', in Ellacuría and Sobrino (eds), *Mysterium Liberationis Fundamental Concepts of Liberation Theology*, pp. 57–85 at p. 67.

26 Vattimo, *After Christianity*, p. 2.

27 Maritain also became important for Latin American liberation theologians, particularly for the first generation of those who studied in France such as Juan Luis Segundo SJ and Gustavo Gutiérrez; see Enrique D. Dussel, 1993, 'Theology of Liberation and Marxism', in Ellacuría and Sobrino (eds), *Mysterium Liberationis Fundamental Concepts of Liberation Theology*, pp. 85–102, at p. 87.

28 Vattimo, *After Christianity*, p. 15.

29 Vattimo, *After Christianity*, p. 97.

30 I have relied for these biographical notes on Santiago Zabala, 2007, 'Introduction: Gianni Vattimo and Weak Philosophy', in Santiago Zabala (ed.), *Weakening Philosophy: Essays in Honour of Gianni Vattimo*, Montreal and Kingston: McGill-Queen's University Press, pp. 3–34, at pp. 26–7.

31 Paolo Flores D'Arcais, 2007, 'Gianni Vattimo; or rather, Hermeneutics as the Primacy of Politics', in Zabala (ed.), *Weakening Philosophy*, pp. 250–69, at p. 250.

32 Fernando Armindo Lugo Méndez was elected President of Paraguay in the 2008 presidential elections. Lugo joined a Catholic missionary congregation, the Divine Word Missionaries, when he was 19 years of age and he was ordained as a priest on 15 August 1977. After five years as a missionary in Ecuador, he returned to Paraguay; however, the Paraguayan government pushed for his expulsion from the country and Lugo was sent for further studies in Rome where he read sociology. In 1987, he returned to Paraguay and on 17 April 1994 he was consecrated bishop of the diocese of San Pedro, one of the poorest in the country. On 11 January 2005, he resigned his post to run a political campaign representing the poor and the only credible challenge to the Partido Colorado, the only successful party in government of Paraguay. He was elected president of Paraguay on 20 April 2008. Lugo's campaign for land reform and the indigenous populations of Paraguay caught the political imagination of Latin America; however, it was an example of an ongoing close relation between the churches and the indigenous populations vis-à-vis the long-term government of General Alfredo Stroessner (1954–89); see René D. Harder Horst, 2007, *The*

Stroessner Regime and Indigenous Resistance in Paraguay, Gainesville, FL: University Press of Florida.

33 Teresa Oñate, 2007, 'The Rights of God in Hermeneutical Postmodernity', in Zabala (ed.), *Weakening Philosophy*, pp. 369–86, at p. 383.

34 See for example, Leonardo Boff, 2006, *Fundamentalism, Terrorism and the Future of Humanity*, London: SPCK.

35 In the case of the United States, the humanitarian intervention without UN consent developed by the Clinton administration prepared for the 2003 invasion of Iraq and the so-called 'war on terror'. In the immediate aftermath of 9/11 a nation united in grief the powers of the US president and the intervention in cases of kidnapping of suspects, and 'rendition' created the possibility of new critiques of the actual moral and ethical powers of President George W. Bush. See Peter R. Gathje, 2007, 'Speaking the Truth to the Power of the Presidency', *Political Theology* 8 (2007/4), pp. 483–92. Cf. Stanley Hauerwas and Frank Lentricchia (eds), 2002, *Dissent from the Homeland: Essays after September 11*, Durham, NC and London: Duke University Press.

36 Leonardo Boff, 2007, 'Two Urgent Utopias for the Twenty-First Century', in Althaus-Reid, Petrella and Susin (eds), *Another Possible World*, pp. 4–9, at p. 4.

37 Wanda Deifelt, 2007, 'Social Context, Language and Images of God', in Althaus-Reid, Petrella and Susin (eds), *Another Possible World*, pp. 118–30, at p. 120.

38 Judith M. Brown (ed.), 2008, *Mahatma Gandhi: The Essential Writings*, Oxford: Oxford University Press, § 76. Originally published in *Young India* 11 September 1924.

39 Robert Mickens wrote 'in revising the text for the recently restored Tridentine Rite, the Pope disappointed many people by leaving untouched a petition that all Jews be converted to Christianity'. See 'Pope orders change in Tridentine prayer for Jews', *The Tablet*, 9 February 2008, p. 29.

40 *Nostra aetate* § 5.

41 Claude Geffré, OP, 2007, 'The Future of Religion: Between Fundamentalism and Modernity', in Althaus-Reid, Petrella and Susin (eds), *Another Possible World*, pp. 39–51, at p. 41.

6

Inter-Religions and a Common Humanity

In the previous chapter the absence of God during a genocidal period was replenished theologically by examining the central tenet of human life and the central tenet of Christianity: love. If the Rwandan genocide and the Jewish Holocaust in Europe had something in common it was the absence of love and the hate expressed through political laws against human beings. Vattimo argued that love remains at the centre of a common life in philosophical terms; he also argued that 'there is no alternative model of Christian life apart from the historical and always contingent involvement required of all the faithful; there is no arcane knowledge of the mysteries that might be foreclosed to non-believers'.[1] Thus, love and the practice of every religion, particularly Christianity, do not see knowledge or esoteric knowledge as central to faithful activity but as at the higher level of a commandment of love towards God and neighbour. It is through this commandment that one can understand the greatness of the Christian call and at the same time the understandable failure of Christianity in Rwanda. For behind any genocide and any conflict there is a failure to love one's neighbour and to love all.

Love, in this sense, becomes a unique Christian commitment and way of life while connecting at the same time with the universal and commonly humane love for those whom one loves dearly to the exclusion of others. Christian love as correctly lived excludes no one and loves everyone. And most importantly, in the words of Paul, 'love never comes to an end' (1 Cor. 13.8). Genocide becomes a denial of a God of life because, as Gustavo Gutiérrez reminds us, 'God is someone who self-manifests within history and, at the same time, is present in the heart of each individual'.[2] In taking part or collaborating with genocide human beings reject the possibility of God's acceptance by human beings because they have rejected the possibility of loving others, including those they did not know personally or those who were different from them.

This chapter expands the possibilities of love and theologizing within a larger world, a globalized one. The history of Rwanda is our history and the history of all and the theological concerns for love and liberation after genocide are the concerns of a larger humanity, a renewed ethical commitment to love.[3] The construction of genocidal structures required the demonization of others, the common understanding that others are not part of us and that because they threaten our very existence they must be eliminated. The Jews were unworthy of living because they threatened the purity of the German state, the Communists were unworthy of living because they threatened the Western civilized model of the military regimes, the Tutsis were unworthy of living because they were sub-human, prey to be hunted, caught and killed. I have expressed many times my own personal experience of the rise of nationalism and militarism in Latin America, a phenomenon that gave rise to a hunt of undesirable human beings by arguing that the basis of violence is a strong nationalism and that the basis of war, conflict and genocide lies in nationalism out of control. This is a discussion that was central to the first centuries of Christian practice and while it was agreed that Christians should take part in human endeavours, societies and nations it was also agreed that Christians had Christ as their ultimate master over the power of the state and particularly those who used the power of government to oppress others.

In the twenty-first century and after the genocides in Rwanda and the Balkans it has become clear that nations preoccupied with their national security after 9/11 have fuelled distrust against the Muslim community because most of the agents of international terrorism have spoken of their Muslim convictions using a misconception of the *jihad* (the holy war) that for most Muslim commentators refers to the acceptance of the One God, of Mohammed as the Prophet, and the interior and spiritual fight to discard all other preoccupations. As a result of the distrust of Islam by Western nations and the implicit distrust of inter-religious dialogue by Pope Benedict XVI the possibilities of hate and confrontation have increased.[4] The common work of helping others by several world religions working together has been in some cases replaced by anger and by questions about the central tenets of a faith community as if others could be the judges of sacred texts and particular interpretations of an evolving religious tradition. The ultimate criticisms of Islam have come from scholars of Islam such as Bernard Lewis who in his historical analysis of Islam and the West argues that Islam is not able to modernize because it is not able to separate religion and politics, whereas Christianity has become part of a Western civilization without impeding a process of European Enlightenment.[5] For Lewis' argument of a clash of civilizations, following previous debates in the United States, does not provide a thorough examination of the history of Islam so that Lewis' analysis, in the words of Marcel Poorthuis, 'degenerates into a regurgitation of his own personal political convictions and to a rather populist view of culture'.[6]

An example of this closeness of European discussions on Islam after 9/11 in the United States and 7/7 in the United Kingdom was the general controversy aroused by the Archbishop of Canterbury in February 2008 when he raised the question about the possibility of using some aspects of Islamic law in the United Kingdom. Most of his critics thought that he was behaving like an academic (he previously was an Oxford University professor) rather than a religious leader and even within some quarters of the Anglican Church there were calls for his resignation.[7] However, other Christian denominations supported his right to ask questions and to raise the possibility that parts of a religious body of law could be more pertinent for a particular faith community, particularly within a nation in which the church is established but where in practice more credibility and voice is given to what Clifford Longley has called 'self-serving secularism'.[8] There is no doubt that in the case of the Catholic Church and despite the fact that divorce is legal in the United Kingdom Catholics who have married following Catholic Canon Law require a different legal tribunal in order to annul their marriage and cannot be satisfied solely by dissolving their union in civil law. That was pointed out as a difficulty within Islamic law by Mona Siddiqui who reminded faith communities and the secularized realm of society that 'laws are not made in a vacuum; there is always a social and moral context'.[9] However, the churches welcomed the possibility of engaging in interfaith dialogue by asking very pertinent questions about the role of religious laws within contemporary society and the possibility of an alliance of faiths that could point a way forward. Thus, Canon Chancellor Chris Chivers of Blackburn Cathedral was quick to point to the enhancement of Rwandan law after the 1994 genocide through the functioning of 'the *gacaca* courts in Rwandan villages, established to hear cases relating to the genocide – [they] represent a tremendous enhancement not a diminishment of the rule of law'.[10]

Christianity and Buddhism

In the previous chapter, I explored the possibility of a renewed encounter with contemporary European philosophy; in this chapter I propose to explore liberation theology as a catalyst of an absence not of God but of genocide vis-à-vis love and liberation within world religions and particularly within Buddhism. The choice of Buddhism rather than Hinduism is a personal choice informed by the possibilities of religious commonality as Buddhism uses the expression 'liberation' in order to maintain a possibility of becoming detached from material and emotional attachments that hinder the acceptance of suffering and ongoing compassion towards all sentient beings. In the context of India, for example, Francis X. D'Sa has explored the possible commonalities and difficulties of the concept of incarnation within a Hindu context and the concept of *avatara* 'when the divine descends into this world and becomes present in one form (= nature) or another'.[11]

Dialogue with Buddhism was already affirmed by Vatican II as follows: 'Buddhism in its various forms testifies to the essential inadequacy of this changing world. It proposes a way of life by which men can, with confidence and trust, attain a state of perfect liberation and reach supreme illumination either through their own efforts or by the aid of divine help.'[12] I must admit that am not absolutely sure that dialogue is the right word because in most cases it has implied a conversation about reality rather than a common search for human and divine truths that arise out of actions, in this case the action of being religious. In this sense interreligious dialogue needs the same hermeneutics that came out of liberation theology: dialogue is a second step, common action for the poor and marginalized comes first. In the words of Vatican II: 'ever aware of her [the Church] desire to foster unity and charity among individuals, and even among nations. She [the Church] reflects at the outset on what men [and women] have in common and what tends to promote fellowship among them'.[13] Thus, in this chapter I am less concerned with agreements or disagreements on religious or philosophical truths; I am deeply concerned by the challenge of liberation, love and the absence of genocide through a common path, a common pilgrimage and a common humanity where the biblical truth of creation is uphold: God created human beings in his own image and therefore we are all precious and equal in the eyes of God.[14] That is before theology divided us and suffering reunited each to other once again.

It is clear that some of the most prominent Asian Christian theologians have been influenced by their own encounter, study and dialogue with Buddhism.[15] I follow Kenneth Fleming's choice here when he argued that Kosuke Koyama, Choan-Seng Song and Aloysius Pieris 'have all engaged in a significant dialogue with Buddhism that has influenced their theologies'.[16] Those Christian theologians in different ways have not only been immersed in their own contextual encounter with Buddhist communities but they have not feared the possibilities of learning and engaging with Buddhist practitioners.[17] The closest Asian theology to a Latin American liberation theology has certainly been that of Pieris because he argued for the liberation of Asia, with its religious diversity and its poverty, through the liberation of Christian theology as well as interreligious dialogue. According to Fleming 'rather than speak of salvation in terms of a relationship with God, liberation is described and defined by him with language that stresses the inner conversion of the individual to become a selfless and greedless person, and the transformation of the social order from injustice to one of love and justice'.[18]

It is at this theological juncture that a very important encounter between Thomas Merton and the fourteenth Dalai Lama remains central to contemporary theology. Merton, a respected Christian writer and contemplative, visited the fourteenth Dalai Lama in India in 1968 and as a result the Dalai Lama expressed his own surprise at meeting, for the first time, a Christian with whom he could exchange views on God, the world, the monastic life, meditation and the practice of religion within a difficult period of history, in which as today the United States was fighting against the 'other', i.e. the Communist forces during the Vietnam War. In a moment of intense global conflict in which the United States and the Soviet Union distrusted each other's aims, two great spiritual leaders met to discuss their commonality at a time when ecumenism within the Christian churches was just starting at official level and further dialogue with other world religions was not central to anybody's agenda. This encounter remains of enormous theological importance because it set the agenda for future encounters between diverse peoples and leaders and the fourteenth Dalai Lama as the religious leader of all Tibetan Buddhists. It is important to note that during the period of the British colonial empire before India's independence there was a general sense that Asia offered a multitude of religious experiences. It was and it is still suggested that 'most people go to India to find themselves' and Thomas Merton was no exception to that proposition.[19]

Thomas Merton and the Fourteenth Dalai Lama

Merton's opening to the contemporary issues that challenged Catholicism in the 1960s was triggered by his avid spiritual and intellectual curiosity but was supported by the climate of opening to other religions discussed at the Second Vatican Council. There is no doubt that in exploring the stranger Merton found an affirmation of his own contentment with a monastic life; his search for other ways of encountering God or the monastic experience associated with Buddhism affirmed him in his own vocation. This monastic contentment on the part of Merton did not assume spiritual stagnation but a continuous challenge to the possibility of a non-changeable Cistercian way of life and Merton's unfailing support for other ways of monasticism, particularly those suggested and later implemented by Merton's former novice, Ernesto Cardenal, in Nicaragua.[20] Indeed, Merton disliked formality and the formalism of even the new documents of renewal that were coming out of Vatican II. For example, during October 1964, the readings in the refectory of the Abbey of Gethsemani included the *Bulletin of the Liturgical Commission and the Congregation of Rites* related to liturgical changes for the 1965 season of Lent. Merton liked the liturgical changes but after the reading of such a formal liturgical document asked 'How can we have "renewal" with such elaborate formalities as this?'[21]

Immediately after the Second Vatican Council, Merton took to heart the call to dialogue with other world religions and corresponded with Asian scholars and religious practitioners, encouraged by the Japanese scholar Daisetz Teitaro Suzuki (1870–1966), who had through many lectures interpreted Zen Buddhism to the West and Christianity to the East. Thus, Merton had read extensively on Zen and Buddhism in general and corresponded with scholars of Hinduism and Buddhism as well.[22] Both Merton and the Dalai Lama became part of a Western religious imagination searching for peace and change. What both had in common was their sense of exile, in the case of the Dalai Lama away from his Tibetan land since 1959; in the case of Merton, a person with no roots anywhere and who had found his home at the Abbey of Gethsemani after escaping enlistment as a US soldier in 1941 due to bad health. By that time, after a long search for meaning in his life, Merton had become a Catholic and had entered the Abbey of Gethsemani in the US state of Kentucky.

By the time of his unfortunate death in Thailand on 10 December 1968, Thomas Merton had become the most important Catholic intellectual in the United States and a revered figure within the peace movement. Despite the fact that he was so active in corresponding with and supporting peace activists and those involved in interfaith dialogue he was a member of the Order of Cistercians of the Strict Observance (Trappists) and had lived as a contemplative monk at the Abbey of Gethsemani in Kentucky for 27 years.[23]

Merton's trip to Asia came about through an invitation extended by a Benedictine group that was helping to implement renewal throughout the world as required by the Second Vatican Council. The idea was to gather in a conference all Asian monastic leaders, including Benedictine and Cistercian leaders, in Bangkok (Thailand) in December 1968. Merton also agreed to give an address to the Spiritual Summit Conference in Calcutta and to give a series of talks at different monasteries in Asia. However, he wanted to visit as many Buddhist monasteries as possible so that according to his secretary, Brother Patrick Hart, 'Thomas Merton's pilgrimage to Asia was an effort on his part to deepen his own religious and monastic commitment'.[24]

Merton had a sustained interest in Asian monasticism and had read extensively on Zen and Buddhism in general.[25] It is possible to argue that, had he not died in December 1968, Merton would have done groundbreaking work in interfaith Christian–Buddhist relations. His Asian trip was authorized by his abbot so as to report back on the possibilities of Cistercian expansion of communities in Asia, despite the fact that Merton's abbot had little confidence in the practicality of Merton as a decision-maker. Previously Merton had explored the possibilities of founding monastic communities in Alaska, but because he had visited during summer he had missed the fact that during winter the visibility due to bad weather and fog was nil. This was probably an example of Merton the intellectual and poet who had less interest in the material practicalities of founding and maintaining monasteries.

By the time that Merton and the fourteenth Dalai Lama met, the Dalai Lama had already become part of the religious imagination of the world due to his flight from Lhasa in March 1959 and his arrival as a refugee in India, highlighting the advancing power of the Chinese Army and the consolidation of the People's Republic of China as a world player in the Cold War. Subsequently Tibetan Buddhist communities started arriving in Western countries and the plight of Tibet within the Cultural Revolution became well known within Europe and the United States. However, at the time of Merton's visit the Dalai Lama was not the world traveller that he became later. It was the conferral of the Nobel Peace Prize in 1989 that brought his message in full force to a Western audience captivated by this monk in robes with a good sense of humour and religious followers everywhere. The Dalai Lama's speech during the Nobel Prize acceptance ceremony highlighted the simplicity and the power of a common humanity.

It is within those conversations and a movement of theological reflection on liberation and interfaith dialogue that I move to some reflections on Asia's religious experience and a renewed question within the theology of the death of God: is it possible to journey with other human beings in the name of God despite the fact that Buddhists, for example, do not believe in a creator being or the God that Christianity proclaims?[26] If for Rwanda and liberation theology the theme and reality of the 'absence of God' or 'the death of God' remains peripheral one must try in a post-genocide situation to face these questions, helped by those traditions and practitioners who are good and faith-oriented despite the fact that they do not believe in a Supreme Creator or a God.

The following reflections rely on the accounts we have of the encounter between Thomas Merton and the Dalai Lama. Throughout his visit Merton wrote a diary that was published later and the highlight of his visit to Asia was the visit to the Dalai Lama and the conferences he gave to other Cistercians and Benedictines.[27] It is striking throughout his diary how Merton was conversant with Buddhist and Sanskrit terminology and how all his conversations related to monastic issues and his search for further solitude. Thus, after days of visiting places and people he could only think that he needed a few days of solitude and because of this maybe the visit to Dharamsala (India), where the headquarters of the Tibetan government in exile and the sacred places associated with the Dalai Lama are still located, became the highlight of his Asian trip.[28]

Merton was brought to the Dalai Lama by Harold Talbott, an American student of Buddhism, who at that time was studying with the Dalai Lama. Talbott had been a student at Harvard University and had become a Catholic. He had made contact with Merton at Gethsemani and had been confirmed at the abbey. Merton stayed at the bungalow that the Dalai Lama had assigned to Talbott and after the meetings with the Dalai Lama Talbott accompanied Merton to Darjeeling where they parted on 24 November 1968.[29]

The meetings took place at the Dalai Lama's quarters in McLeod Ganj, a small Himalayan enclave located on the hills above Dharamsala described by Merton as 'admirably situated, high over the valley, with snow-covered mountains behind, all pine trees, with apes in them, and a vast view over the plains to the south'.[30] As Merton waited to enter the Dalai Lama's meeting room he noticed that there were shelves with Buddhist works presented to the Dalai Lama by his friend D. T. Suzuki.[31] Their first meeting on 4 November 1968 dealt with religion and philosophy and ways of meditating and Merton listened attentively to the importance of Tibetan Buddhism somehow criticized by other more traditional Buddhist schools of thought and practice.[32] Merton's knowledge of Tibetan Buddhism must have been good because they discussed *dzogchen*, the 'great perfection', the Great Way of All-inclusiveness, the esoteric tradition of the Nyingmapas order of Tibetan Buddhism, a tradition that goes back to the eighth century when great teachers such as Guru Padma Sambhava (Swat Valley) and Vimalamitra (India) visited Tibet. *Dzogchen* constitutes a very direct way to knowledge and the Dalai Lama told Merton 'not to misunderstand the simplicity of *dzogchen*'.[33]

Their second meeting took place on 6 November 1968 and they discussed epistemology and the mind, particularly Tibetan and Western-Thomist theories.[34] Later, they discussed meditation and the Dalai Lama showed Merton the essential position for meditation in Tibetan Buddhism whereby 'the right hand (discipline) is above the left (wisdom)', while in Zen Buddhism it is the other way around.[35] Merton commented on the Dalai Lama's way of thinking as follows: 'I like the solidity of the Dalai Lama's ideas. He is a very consecutive thinker and moves from step to step. His ideas of the interior life are built on very solid foundations and on a real awareness of practical problems.'[36]

Their third meeting took place on 8 November 1968 when they discussed Western monastic life, vows, dietary prohibitions etc.[37] Merton raised the point of monasticism and Marxism, the topic of his Bangkok lecture, and the Dalai Lama, who admired Marxism, suggested that 'from a certain point of view it was impossible for monks and Communists to get along, but that perhaps it should not be entirely impossible *if* Marxism meant *only* the establishment of an equitable economic and social structure'.[38] It is clear that Merton's diaries only provide a short sketch of their conversations and that the actual sense of a personal conversation is missing for the reader and would have been expanded by Merton later in writings and conferences. However, it is possible to suggest that at the end of Merton's conversations with the Dalai Lama there was a natural closeness and a spiritual bond between them. Later, the Dalai Lama in his own autobiography recognized that the death of Merton had deprived the world of the possibility of a meaningful dialogue between Christians and Buddhists with all their similarities.[39] Nevertheless, it is clear that the meetings between Merton and the Dalai Lama had provided a sign of Vatican II's clear statement to the effect that all human beings 'form but one community'.[40]

When in 1995 the Dalai Lama visited Merton's grave at Gethsemani, he meditated in front of Merton's grave accompanied by Abbot Timothy Kelly OCSO.[41] Thus, three decades later the conversation between Merton and the Dalai Lama was resumed in the words of Tenzin Gyatso: 'I am now in touch with his spirit'.[42] The fact is that the conversations about the spiritual path that had taken place between Merton and the Dalai Lama made them aware of *a common spiritual experience*. The commonality did not come from the possibility of discussing notions of a divine being, as Buddhists do not uphold creation out of an act by a divine being, but from a notion of emptiness. The spiritual emptiness of a Buddhist monk and that of a Cistercian monk lies on the act of self-emptying. For the Buddhist the emptying conduces to an awareness of the power of the mind in fostering enlightenment and in the particular case of Tibetan Buddhists such an emptying conduces to an attitude of compassion and communion with all sentient beings, human and animal alike. This point is rather poignant at a time when ecological issues and a theology of creation is at the front of the Christian reflection of a globalized community suffering the perils of global warming and the depletion of the planet's natural resources.

Religious Dialogue as Theological Manifestation

Let me reflect on some of the ideas and attitudes that arise out of Merton's conversation with the Dalai Lama in general and between Christians and Buddhists in particular. First, a common spiritual experience did not mean that their contexts and paths were identical but that Merton and the Dalai Lama shared the common call of all human beings to acknowledge a spiritual path and a spiritual experience that makes all human beings share *a common path through different contexts*. This common call is expressed in the Buddhist compassion for all sentient beings and in the Christian love for all human beings, both realized through the hospitality shown by members of monastic communities to visitors, merely strangers in need of affirmation and in need of human examples of an appreciation of a spiritual world that becomes real and tangible through the experience of practitioners. Practitioners such as Merton do not solely show *the kindness and compassion to strangers* but in doing so over a period of time minimize and finally destroy the possibility of perceiving other human beings as 'strangers'.

Second, it is important to remember that the word liberation is used by Christian theologians as well as by Buddhists. Theologians of liberation developed the central tenet of their practice of Christianity by suggesting that Christian orthodoxy resided within a Christian orthopraxis; Tibetan Buddhists have described the same way of personal liberation from suffering. Thus, if Gustavo Gutiérrez expressed his solidarity with the poor in the name of God by actualizing the possibility of human liberation from poverty and underdevelopment, the Dalai Lama in his teaching has also used liberation from suffering as a human goal. For in Tibetan Buddhism there are two ways of attaining some merit in order to aspire towards a good means of reincarnation: the field of the Buddhas and the field of other sentient beings. Thus, the field of merit related to other sentient beings 'involves practicing actions like kindness, generosity, tolerance, and so on, and conscious restraint from negative actions like killing, stealing, and lying'.[43]

Thus, within these parameters of relatedness between the message of the Gospels and the Tibetan Buddhist scriptures it is possible to argue once again that it is the systematic rigid reflection on truth and ontology, as outlined by Vattimo, explored in the previous chapter, that creates a crisis between diverse theologies in the world religions. This crisis always arises if theology comes as the first movement of a human being who is trying to understand the contemporary world and God's action within a world that he created.

The contemporary situation of the world indicates that Asia in general and China in particular have taken centre-stage in the cooperation between the West and the arising economic powers of the East, India and China. The Western focus on the growth of Christianity in Asia has still the signs of the evangelical crusades and the missionary movement of the nineteenth century in that finally the East seems open for a full movement of evangelization. This would be a missed opportunity if we miss 'the signs of the time'. In 2008, the Jesuits elected a new Superior General. Adolfo Nicolás, a Spaniard, had 40 years of experience in Asia, and had always said that the whole Church has a lot to learn from Asia. In the words of Felix Wilfred,

> I think this is the contribution Adolfo is taking to Rome at a time when Asian theology for many looks like an enfant terrible, disquieting the Church with its strange ideas and theological positions. I surmise that he will say to the central administration of the Church in Rome that there need not be any exaggerated fear about Asia.[44]

It is my contention that Asia remains the place where the twenty-first century will find a full encounter of an African, Latin American and Asian theology of liberation. There at the current periphery of the ecclesiastical world of Europe is where a new ecclesiology will arise in the dialogue with the greater depths of a liberated humanity, rather than from the depths of a new ecclesiastical order or an evangelical crusade.[45] I return to the difficult areas of a renewed ecclesiology because it is a constant critique of our theological tenets that provides the possibility of liberation and not just of theologies of liberation within texts and academia. The movement from the centre to the periphery remains a central tenet for liberation theology because when any theology becomes part of the centre and the accepted establishment it loses its reason for existence: to accompany the poor and the marginalized in their own journey with God, who after all shows them his preference.

I cannot deny that this possible interreligious dialogue outside the confines of European and scholastic paradigms of interpretation and expansion on 'truth' leads us once again to the questioning of current trends and structures of the churches and to the rethinking of an ecclesiology that dominates the life of the churches today. I agree again with Leonardo Boff's assessment of an early Christian ecclesiology when he wrote that the Church 'exists in the form of mystery, which is the manner of existence of God: above and beyond all limits and determinations whatever'.[46] The commandment of love that embraces the sinner as well as the saved urges us to think theologically about God the Liberator and his plan for his creation during the twenty-first century. The hermeneutics of bones can suggest that God is present in moments of human collapse and maintains his support in moments in which love seems to be totally absent. I have already suggested in my evaluation of the history of Latin American theology that it was when the followers of Christ took to heart the presence of God among the poor and the marginalized that the communities emerged with an uncompromising message of love and compassion. The movement to the periphery of society becomes a new Exodus that cannot be avoided at a time when the media want us to believe that globalization will provide a safe world with all commodities available.[47] The economic instability and the rising price of oil in 2008 has already reminded us that no economic structure or consumerist dream can bring the joy and fulfilment of being totally human, in a constant journey with God, and this at the peripheries of the world. It is the love of God and neighbour and the experience of a common humanity that will bring an absence of war, of hatred and of genocide; an experience that also requires solidarity with the poor and the constant involvement in building a just society based on the values of the Kingdom of God. After the question of a post-genocidal theology is the question already uttered by David Power: 'In the wake of mass death, how do a people learn to look to a future when justice may be be done to the dead as well as the living?' so that 'remembering can carry a new potential for life in the remembrance of those who have perished'.[48]

Notes

1 Gianni Vattimo, 2002, *After Christianity*, New York: Columbia University Press, p. 136.

2 Gustavo Gutiérrez, 1991, *The God of Life*, London: SCM Press, p. xiii.

3 Mario I. Aguilar, 1998, *The Rwanda Genocide and the Call to Deepen Christianity in Africa*, Eldoret, Kenya: AMECEA Gaba Publications.

4 I am not arguing here that Pope Benedict XVI is completely opposed to interreligious dialogue but that he has brought it back to an intellectual level of formal visits and academic conferences departing from the active encouragement to local churches and the active participation in interfaith dialogue supported by Pope John Paul II. In stressing Christianity as the only source of Western civilization, he has made interfaith dialogue more difficult and the possible construction of multiculturalism in Europe impossible. See, for example, Joseph Ratzinger, 2004, 'Über den Selbsthaß Europas', *Avenire*, 14 May 2004.

5 Bernard Lewis, 2002, *What Went Wrong? Western Impact and Middle Eastern Response*, Oxford: Oxford University Press.

6 Marcel Poorthuis, 2005, 'What Went Wrong with Bernard Lewis? The Uncertain Debate about Islam and the Enlightenment', in Erik Borgman and Pim Valkenberg (eds), *Islam and Enlightenment New Issues* (*Concilium* 2005/5), London: SCM Press, pp. 23–31, at p. 31.

7 The criticism that Rowan Williams is more a thinker than a leader has been there since he was appointed Archbishop of Canterbury: see Theo Hobson, 'Quiet voice of modernity's enemy', *The Tablet*, 16 February 2008, pp. 4–5, see also Theo Hobson, 2007, *Against Establishment: An Anglican Polemic*, London: Darton, Longman & Todd.

8 Clifford Longley, 'The job of religions', *The Tablet*, 16 February 2008, pp. 6–7.

9 Mona Siddiqui, 'Where sharia can seem problematic is in laws of personal status especially marriage', *The Tablet*, 16 February 2008, p. 9.

10 Chris Chivers, 'Wise and helpful words', *The Tablet*, 16 February 2008, pp.8–9, at p. 9.

11 Francis X. D'Sa, 1993, 'Christian Incarnation and Hindu Avatara', in Leonardo Boff and Virgil Elizondo (eds), *Any Room for Christ in Asia?* (*Concilium* 1993/2), London: SCM Press and Maryknoll, NY: Orbis, pp. 77–85, at p. 79. For a fuller treatment of some aspects of Christian theology and Hinduism see Francis X. D'Sa, 1987, *Gott, der Dreieine und der All-Ganze: Vorwort zur Begegnung zwischen Christentum und Hinduismus*, Düsseldorf: Theologie Interkulturell.

12 *Nostra aetate* § 2.

13 *Nostra aetate* § 1.

14 *Nostra aetate* § 1.

15 For an overview of other approaches to liberation in Asian theology see Bastiaan Wielenga, 1999, 'Liberation Theology in Asia', in Christopher Rowland (ed.), *The Cambridge Companion to Liberation Theology*, Cambridge: Cambridge University Press, pp. 39–62.

16 Kenneth Fleming, 2002, *Asian Christian Theologians in Dialogue with Buddhism*, Bern: Peter Lang.

17 See works by Kosuke Koyama, 1974, *Water Buffalo Theology*, London: SCM Press, *Three Mile an Hour God*, London: SCM Press, 1979 and *Mount Fiji and Mount Sinai: A Pilgrimage in Theology*, London: SCM Press, 1984; by Choan-Seng Song, 1982, *The Compassionate God: An Exercise in the Theology of Transposition*, London: SCM Press, *Tell Us Our Names: Story Theology from an Asian Perspective*, Maryknoll, NY: Orbis, 1984, *Theology from the Womb of Asia*, Maryknoll, NY: Orbis, 1986, *Jesus, the Crucified People*, New York: Crossroad, 1990 and Minneapolis: Fortress Press, 1996, *Third-Eye Theology: Theology in Formation in Asian Settings*, Maryknoll, NY: Orbis, 1991, *Jesus and the Reign of God*, Minneapolis: Fortress Press, 1994, and *The Believing Heart: An Invitation to Story Theology*, Minneapolis: Fortress Press, 1999; by Aloysius Pieris, 1988, *An Asian Theology of Liberation*, Maryknoll, NY: Orbis, *Love Meets Wisdom: A Christian Experience of Buddhism*, Maryknoll, NY: Orbis, 1988, and *Fire and Water: Basic Issues in Asian Buddhism and Christianity*, Maryknoll, NY: Orbis, 1996.

18 Fleming, *Asian Christian Theologians*, p. 210.

19 Dave Lauridsen, 'The Marrying Kind', *The Guardian Weekend*, 21 June 2008, pp. 32–41, at p. 32; see also Anita Jain, 2008, *Marrying Anita: A Quest for Love in the New India*, London: Bloomsbury.

20 See ongoing correspondence between Cardenal and Merton in *Del Monasterio al Mundo: Correspondencia entre Ernesto Cardenal y Thomas Merton*, Santiago, Chile: Editorial Cuarto Propio, 1998 and materials related to the experimental lay contemplative community founded by Cardenal on the Nicaraguan island of Solentiname in Ernesto Cardenal, *El Evangelio en Solentiname*, Salamanca: Ediciones Sígueme, 1976 and *El Evangelio en Solentiname: Volumen Segundo*, Salamanca: Ediciones Sígueme, 1978, see also Mario I. Aguilar, 2007, *The History and Politics of Latin American Theology*, vol. 1, London: SCM Press, chapter 5, pp. 91–104.

21 30 October 1964 in Robert E. Daggy (ed.), 1997, *Dancing in the Water of Life: Seeking Peace in The Hermitage*, The Journals of Thomas Merton, vol. 5, 1963–65, New York: HarperSanFrancisco, p. 159.

22 See, for example, William Apel, 2006, 'There Comes a Time: The Interfaith Letters of Thomas Merton and Dona Luisa Coomaraswamy', *The Merton Journal* 13 (2006/2), pp. 11–18, *Signs of Peace: The Interfaith Letters of Thomas Merton*, Maryknoll, NY: Orbis, 2006 and 'Letters to Sister Therese Lentfoehr SDS', p. 20.

23 For a history of the Abbey of Gethsemani see Dianne Aprile, 1998, *The Abbey of Gethsemani: Place of Peace and Paradox*, Louisville, KY: Trout Lilly Press; for the history of the Cistercians see Esther De Waal, 1998, *The Way of Simplicity: The Cistercian Tradition*, Maryknoll, NY: Orbis, James France, 1998, *The Cistercians in Medieval Art*, Kalamazoo, Michigan: Cistercian Publications, Louis Lekai, 1977, *The Cistercians: Ideals and Reality*, Kent, Ohio: Kent State University Press, André Louf, 1983, *The Cistercian Way*, Kalamazoo, Michigan: Cistercian Publications and Patricia Matarasso (ed.), 1993, *The Cistercian World: Monastic Writings of the Twelfth Century*, London: Penguin.

24 Brother Patrick Hart, 1975, 'Foreword', in *The Asian Journal of Thomas Merton*, New York: New Directions, p. xxiii.

25 During the 1960s, Merton had corresponded with many scholars of Hinduism and Buddhism; see for example, Apel, 'There Comes a Time', pp. 11–18 and *Signs of Peace*.

26 It is beyond the scope of this work to expand on all the principles of Buddhism as a religious and philosophical system and I recommend to the reader any introduction to Buddhism, for example, Rupert Gethin, 1998, *The Foundations of Buddhism*, Oxford and New York: Oxford University Press.

27 Diary notes published as *The Asian Journal of Thomas Merton*, New York: New Directions, 1975.

28 The fourteenth Dalai Lama, Tenzin Gyatso, was born into a peasant family in Amdo, eastern Tibet in 1935 and after being identified as the incarnation of the previous Dalai Lama at the age of two he was moved to Lhasa at the age of four. With the Chinese occupation of Tibet the political situation changed and after the Tibetan National Uprising on the 10 March 1959, the Dalai Lama left Tibet and moved to India where he was given refugee status. Over the years, thousands of Tibetan refugees crossed into India and the Dalai Lama managed to establish monasteries as well as his government in Dharamsala where he met Merton in 1968. For a detailed account of the Dalai Lama's life see Michael Harris Goodman, 1986, *The Last Dalai Lama: A Biography*, London: Sidgwick and Jackson.

29 See 'Talbott, Harold', in William H. Shannon, Christine M. Bochen and Patrick F. O'Connell, *The Thomas Merton Encyclopedia*, Maryknoll, NY: Orbis, 2002, p. 462.

30 *The Asian Journal of Thomas Merton*, p. 100. The same description of the meetings as published in Merton's *Asian Journal* has been also included in the last volume of Merton's personal diaries, see Patrick Hart OCSO (ed.), 1998, *The Other Side of the Mountain: The End of the Journey*, The Journals of Thomas Merton, vol. 7, 1967–68, New York: HarperSanFrancisco, pp. 249–66.

31 Daisetz Teitaro Suzuki (1870–1966) was a Japanese scholar who interpreted Buddhism, and particularly Zen Buddhism, to the West and Christianity to the East. Merton met him in 1964 when Zuzuki lectured at Columbia University; see 'Zen' in William H. Shannon, Christine M. Bochen and Patrick F. O'Connell, *The Thomas Merton Encyclopedia*, pp. 546–8.

32 'November 4/Afternoon', in *The Asian Journal of Thomas Merton*, pp. 100–102.

33 *The Asian Journal of Thomas Merton*, p. 102.

34 *The Asian Journal of Thomas Merton*, pp. 112–13.

35 *The Asian Journal of Thomas Merton*, p. 112.

36 *The Asian Journal of Thomas Merton*, p. 113.

37 *The Asian Journal of Thomas Merton*, pp. 124–5.

38 *The Asian Journal of Thomas Merton*, p. 125. On the Dalai Lama and Marxism see The 14th Dalai Lama, 1990, *Freedom in Exile: The Autobiography of His Holiness the Dalai Lama of Tibet*, London: Hodder & Stoughton, pp. 98–9, 251 and particularly p. 296, where he confesses that 'in as much as I have any political allegiance, I suppose I am still half Marxist' and 'the other

attractive thing about Marxism for me is its assertion that man is ultimately responsible for his own destiny. This reflects Buddhist thought exactly.'

39 The Dalai Lama writes about 'Father Thomas Merton, the American Benedictine Monk', see The 14th Dalai Lama, *Freedom in Exile*, pp. 207–8. See also Joseph Quinn Raab, 2006, 'Comrades for Peace: Thomas Merton, The Dalai Lama and the Preferential Option for Nonviolence', in Victor A. Kramer and David Belcastro (eds), *The Merton Annual: Studies in Culture, Spirituality and Social Concerns* 19, Louisville, KY: Fons Vitae, pp. 255–66.

40 *Nostra aetate* §1, cf. Acts 17.26.

41 Photograph available in William H. Shannon, Christine M. Bochen and Patrick F. O'Connell, *The Thomas Merton Encyclopedia*, p. 99.

42 'Dalai Lama (Tenzin Gyatso)', in William H. Shannon, Christine M. Bochen and Patrick F. O'Connell, *The Thomas Merton Encyclopedia*, pp. 98–9, at p. 99.

43 HH Dalai Lama and Howard C. Cutler, 1999, *The Art of Happiness: A Handbook for Living*, London: Hodder & Stoughton, p. 55.

44 Felix Wilfred, 2008, 'On the election of a General', in Felix Wilfred, Edmong Tang and Georg Evers (eds), *China and Christianity* (*Concilium* 2008/3), London: SCM Press, pp. 128–31, at pp. 128–9.

45 I refer here to the challenging thoughts of Leonardo Boff when he resigned from the Catholic priesthood; he spoke of two models of church in conflict: that of John XXIII and Vatican II and the other which 'starts from the conviction that the church does not need changes, but order and discipline to achieve an efficient spiritual conquest of modern culture'; see Leonardo Boff, 'I Changed to Stay the Same (Why I Left the Priesthood)', in Boff and Elizondo (eds), *Any Room for Christ in Asia?*, pp. 144–8, at p. 145.

46 Leonardo Boff, 1986, *Ecclesiogenesis: The Base Communities Reinvent the Church*, Maryknoll, NY: Orbis, p. 17.

47 I am aware here that the idea of the Exodus as a liberating paradigm also has its problems; when the Israelites are liberated in other to attain their promised land other peoples are oppressed or killed on their way.

48 David N. Power, 1993, 'Calling Up the Dead', in David Power and Kabasele Lumbala (eds), *The Spectre of Mass Death* (*Concilium* 1993/3), London: SCM Press and Maryknoll, NY: Orbis, pp. 111–20, at p. 112.

Conclusion

Hermeneutical Openings

Theology continues being a 'second step' and action; a liberating praxis comes first. Within that reiteration of the validity of liberation theology this chapter summarizes some of the arguments of this book and outlines the renewed need for the churches to allow for an interfaith dialogue of liberation with others, all within the periphery. For it is in Rwanda as well as in the peripheries of this world that Christianity is growing; it is within those peripheries that God is liberating and that a new liberation theology based on bones as hermeneutical texts is arising. However, the theological readings about the 1994 Rwandan genocide are very clear: the creation of a Christian majority and the establishment of a triumphant and rejoicing church in Rwanda did not prevent one of the worst atrocities in the history of humanity.

The Golden Period

In a recent meeting of Catholic missionaries in Dublin, on the fortieth anniversary of the meeting of Latin American bishops in Medellin (Colombia, 1968), discussions revolved around the significance of liberation theology: was it a moment in the history of the Church or was it a movement? My tentative answer was that it was a *kairos*, a blessed moment in history, not only in the history of the Church that allowed the values of the Kingdom to be highlighted through the praxis of love by the Christian communities. That practice was militant and prophetic in that it questioned the possibility of a given order in society.[1] However, as I have outlined in my analysis of the history of theology in Latin America, that praxis was based on love – love of God and love of neighbour. Thus, when people ask about the past and future of liberation theology they miss the fact that the context of the military regimes ended but the timeless capacity by Christian communities to question and to love remain. Maybe the sense of urgency has changed; the pace is slower and the given fruits less tangible. This is not a sign of an end but of a beginning. It is possible to argue that the church is less visible but it is there; it is possible to acknowledge that fewer theological writings in Spanish or Portuguese are being translated into English but nevertheless those writings do exist.

The first and second generation of liberation theologians such as Gustavo Gutiérrez, Jon Sobrino and Juan Luis Segundo created a body of theological literature that reflected what I would call a golden period with Latin America and indeed within the churches in general and the Catholic Church in particular. It was a time of heightened community efforts for a deeper understanding of the values of the Kingdom of God. It was also a time in which theologians and those working ordinarily to obtain their daily bread were able to share a common understanding of their roles as pilgrims in the same pilgrimage of faith, and of politics. However, there is no doubt that changing winds affected the Christian communities as the absolute truth of Christ became a bastion for conservatism and for orthodoxy during the pontificate of John Paul II, who through the arm of Cardinal Joseph Ratzinger put order rather than creativity within those teaching the Catholic faith at all levels in Latin America.[2] Enough has been written about this.

Rwanda and Latin America share some of the same ecclesial realities, for example the post-traumatic context of trying to deal with the past and with the many dead who constitute parts of families, communities and of the church as a whole. It is my contention in this book that after enormous suffering and trauma the signs of the Kingdom start to come out and more narratives of heroic love for neighbour and enemy are being outlined. However, the liberating praxis of the 'people of God' as Vatican II defines all believers and people of good alike will continue because 'at all times and in every race, anyone who fears God and does what is right has been acceptable to him' (cf. Acts 10.35).[3]

How can we deal with the present and the future theologically? How can we assert the love of God and the understanding of God's support for all human beings today? How can we restore the possibilities of the golden period of liberation theology after the international mistrust caused by the events of 9/11, the war of Iraq and the international intervention in Afghanistan? Rwanda, after the 1994 genocide, becomes once again a possible context in which to reiterate the possibilities and impossibilities faced by liberation theology in the twenty-first century. The issue of the unburied bones of which I have tried to make sense and which has provided a hermeneutical ground for a theological reading of bones has also an oppressive and contradictory aspect. In an epistolary exchange with a Dutch Reformed pastor who worked in Rwanda before and after the genocide (1973–82, 1995–99) I realized that during the post-genocide period the lack of burials in Rwanda has been a forced government policy, an instance of the state fixation with providing reconciliation by force rather than by dialogue and consensus.[4] Gerard van 't Spijker reminded me of his interest in funeral rituals in Rwanda and his conclusion that Rwandans always handled the dead carefully, with enormous care and with love.[5] Further, he suggests that ways of dealing with the dead in a communal manner have changed since the genocide and that the support of the different churches for burials has also changed, becoming a more private matter.[6] However, the fact that the Rwandan government did not allow the burial of thousands of corpses in order to pursue a state agenda of national reconciliation has been questioned by Rwandans interviewed by Gerard van 't Spijker and the institution of a week of national mourning by the Rwandan government has been described by others, for example anthropologist Claudine Vidal, as 'one of the cruelties of the present regime'.

It is here that we must pause in order to suggest that state polities and societal happenings cannot be taken, theologically speaking, as *prima facie*. For the role of the liberation theologian remains to question social and state institutions or policies and social realities that create suffering, especially for the poor and the marginalized. We must instead turn to the possibility of God's centrality and the 'insignificant' role of the theologian. After all, any theologian journeys together with all members of the People of God, everybody as outlined by Vatican II. Together, theologians and all others follow the same road, a road which in Rwanda has been filled with corpses as well as hate and dust.

The hermeneutics of bones as a theological device is not a heuristic device for intellectual consumption but a second act, a renewed commitment to the first act, the act of following the journey, of acting in commitment to life, death and God. It is this spirit that may have been forgotten on the roads that led to prosperity and globalization after the collapse of the Berlin Wall in the 1990s. The road to prosperity is one way; the road filled with corpses, with unburied bones, is another way and it is the latter that allows us to get to know God. As I have previously suggested in my poetry, God does not solely support the oppressed, the persecuted, the suffering, the tortured and the electrocuted; God is tortured and electrocuted, as one more of many prisoners, without a name, as we speak.[7]

Interpreting the Bones

The relocation of God to the periphery in Rwanda, outside the churches that became dangerous grounds for killings, suggests that the Rwandan experience connects with the shift from centre to periphery in Latin American theology. Of course we are all part of a common humanity, as Buddhists would say, but this commonality has been forgotten too many times. When churches, hospitals, schools and government buildings cannot offer shelter, the road is the way of shelter. The road of pilgrims and penitents is a road where God walks as one of us. The destination is not the point; what is sought is the actualization of love, prosperity and solidarity on the road. This was the original contribution of liberation theology in its first moment and it constitutes the connection between a theological reflection on Rwanda and on Latin America in the early twenty-first century.

There is no doubt that we all have skeletons in our closets. Jesus himself was a suspect Galilean preaching new things together with a suspect group of disciples also from Galilee. He criticized the institutions of Israel and of the Jews at that time and finally was accused of blasphemy and treason to Rome and the Jewish nation and was crucified. Jesus' road from Galilee of the Gentiles to Jerusalem set the tone for the journey along a theological road littered with corpses and bones. And every bone has a message, every dismembered part of a body has a message of liberation and salvation, every suffering human being on the road represents the incarnate God and the *caminata* of each one of us is a walk through life with God, healing, supporting, liberating, comforting, reflecting, announcing God news.[8]

It is my suggestion that a post-genocidal theology is a theology that allows us to reflect on the centralities of the God of Life because those who have been through enormous tribulations and are still alive only treasure the possibility of being alive in order to embrace their loved ones, to see their children grow, to sit under the mystical trees of a common humanity in order to share the joy of being alive. God is not dead, but some of those on the journey are. God is not waiting somewhere ahead of us, God is located at the periphery. The road of life, littered with bones, is the centre. Finally, I want to see liberation theology become an ongoing reflection, a second act through the journey of life, not awaiting a God who will come or a Kingdom that could be of the other world, but to rejoice with a God who walks on the same road and who gives a hand to those who are tired, beaten up or threatened along the way. The road has friends and strangers but all of them, the whole People of God, are friends of God because God is one of them and we don't know which one.

Let me conclude these theological reflections with a sobering comment made by one of the many Rwandan killers: 'There is no one on the hill who can say to God, eyes closed in prayer, that he never went hunting.'[9] The 'hunt', as a metaphor for the daily killings in Rwanda, is a negative metaphor for the life of all of us. Without critical engagement with life and a life in solidarity with the poor and the marginalized we all become part of a globalized 'hunt' rather than part of a theological journey in which we learn from the crucified and the marginalized. Let me explain this. Because in globalization every job and every promotion is a competition against another person who is also a fellow human being, every peer-review and every process of public accountability becomes a possibility and therefore becomes the possibility of being part of a 'hunt'. The consequences of the Rwandan genocide in a country where most citizens are Christians remind us of the possibilities and impossibilities of losing sight of a theology that tells of the equality of human beings based on the equality of a Trinitarian God.

Finally, a theology of genocide arising out of Rwanda uses memory in order to understand God's ways and the ways of human beings. But it provides a sense of diversity that was denied during the genocide. The God that liberates and the God of Life wants people to have life, not death, but the death of Jesus of Nazareth as well as the death of many of those who suffer today reminds us of the possibilities of God, always present and always here, not in the heavens above.

The Rwandan genocide reminds us that in the depth of horror and in the depth of despair God is present as one of those suffering. There is no 'death of God' paradigm, there is no despair, there is still hope and liberation. I have argued previously in my work on Latin America that the death of Christians is a life without utopia and without hope. I described the blindfolded prisoners at the torture camp of the Villa Grimaldi in Chile as follows:

> They didn't fear death but they feared life without utopia, without a dream, without, without the possibility of a better world. They didn't fear torture but they feared life in a world without beauty, without poetry, without warmth and love, even when their love was mechanized by the possibility of being caught and never to be with them again.[10]

If one uses the shifting historical contexts, the suffering of today's indigenous populations and their cry for retribution by the Latin American states or their demands of sociopolitical inclusion or their assertion of their own human dignity, all those human demands remain part of a road to relocate theologies of liberation from clear bounded ecclesial moments to a shifting context of globalization and, as I have suggested, to the road *of* God, rather than to the road *to* God. One could certainly speak of a journey to an imaginary utopian place that is less defined than in the past. In my aesthetic writings I have called it the road to Waja-Waja for it is on that road that the God of Life is encountered and those who see him are the destitute, the suffering, the poor and the marginalized, for the road to Waja-Waja is filled with spiders that await their prey . . . and God is walking with us towards them.[11]

It is on that road that we will reclaim the God of the poor and the marginalized. In Rwanda in 1994 God was present, hacked with a machete but still with sufficient strength to comfort the dying person next door. All departing missionaries left the road and left God; their duty was to have died there if necessary. But Rwanda today points to a beautiful and hopeful new day. God liberates today in the streets and slums of Santiago where I conclude these remarks on liberation because God is a liberator. But God is not waiting at the top of a beautiful mountain, at the top of the Andes, where he will comfort us. God today is journeying in the same cities of Latin America and in the same hills of Rwanda with dry and wounded hands, with hunger and with pain, with uncertainty and with emotion. The Pinochet genocide of 'communists' or the Rwandan genocide of Tutsis do not speak of the 'death of God' but of the care of God for those who, frail and human, felt at the end of their lives the comfort of a hand and a drop of water being poured on their lips.

At the end a theological bridge joins those involved in praxis and those who are writing academic theology, led always by those involved in theological praxis but necessarily allied to those who can in the name of the Kingdom of God exercise a certain theological advocacy for the poor and the oppressed of this world, so that their voices are heard and their oppression ends on their own terms and according to their own wishes.

Let me end by citing a sobering summary of the killings and the absence of God by a killer called Jean-Baptiste:

> We could not ask time to give us firm deadline for such a long programme. Time seemed to smile on us, desiring only that we no longer worry about God. So we obeyed, and we kept on killing, aiming for the last one. Even though the work went on and on because of the looting and the fatigues of drinking, we never doubted, since no one could stop the work. But God slipped in among the killings to hurry along the *inkotanyi*. In the end God did not accept a definite conclusion – that's the lesson.[12]

Killers and victims returned to the churches, the one group in fear of eternal retribution, the other in hope of love and mercy, an end to horror. However, both groups remain today on the road, on the path where God acts and where God liberates, if he so wishes and whenever he wishes. He never died but was understood to have rested, to have been on a particular side but God was as usual on the wrong side of our understanding. God remained in Rwanda within those who had no hope; those were the ones who were liberated from hatred and from anguish about their fate because they perceived a higher reality: the poor and the marginalized, the victims, are at the centre of God's plan and God's *caminata* through the road of life. God dressed as a beggar leads the *caminata* to the land of Waja-Waja today.

Notes

1 Mario I. Aguilar, 2009, 'The Kairos of Medellín 1968: Towards a Movement for Liberation and New Mission After Vatican II', in Patrick Claffey and Joseph Egan (eds), *Liberation Theology: Movement or Moment?*, Berlin: Peter Lang.

2 Mario I. Aguilar, 2008, 'John Paul II and Theologies of Liberation', in Gerard Mannion (ed.) *The Vision of John Paul II: Assessing His Thought and Influence*, Collegeville, Minnesota: Liturgical Press, pp. 144–58.

3 *Lumen gentium* § 9.

4 Gerard van 't Spijker to Mario I. Aguilar, 11 July 2008.

5 Gerard van 't Spijker, 1990, *Les usages funéraires et la mission de l'Église: Une étude anthropólogique et théologique des rites funéraires au Rwanda*, PhD thesis, Free University of Amsterdam, Kampen: Kok.

6 Gerard van 't Spijker, 2007, *Indicible Rwanda: Expériences et reflexions d'un Pasteur missionaire*, Yaoundé: Editions Clé.

7 'Cantan los prisioneros en la parrilla, cantan nombres de los que serán hallados, cantan nombres queridos y odiados, cantan nombres de cristianos y de moros', Poem V, in Mario Aguilar Benítez, 2008, *A las puertas de la Villa Grimaldi*, Santiago: Caliope Ediciones, p. 18.

8 *Caminata* is the Spanish word for a walk, a longer walk, a symbolic walk, a protest walk, word used within Latin American theology to indicate the process of doing theology within a community and an ongoing walk as a member of a particular community; see Marcella Althaus-Reid, 2004, *From Feminist Theology to Indecent Theology*, London: SCM Press, p. 12 note 1.

9 Jean Hatzfeld, 2005, *A Time for Machetes: The Rwandan Genocide – The Killers Speak*, New York: Farrar, Straus and Giroux and London: Serpent's Tail, p. 66.

10 Mario I. Aguilar, 2008, *The History and Politics of Latin American Theology, vol. 3, A Theology at the Periphery*, London: SCM Press, p. 182.

11 Poem III 'Camino a Waja-Waja', Mario I. Aguilar, 2009, *Pausas: Poemas de Villa Grimaldi a India*, Santiago: Mago Editores, pp. 14–5.

12 Hatzfeld, *A Time for Machetes*, p. 137.

Index